THE WORLD OF EPEISÓDION I

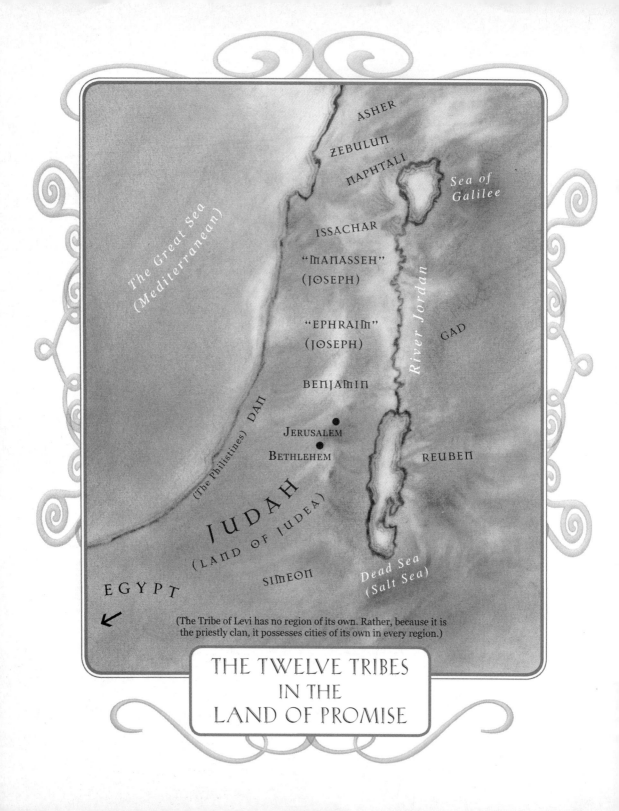

ASHER

ZEBULUN

NAPHTALI

Sea of Galilee

The Great Sea (Mediterranean)

ISSACHAR

"MANASSEH" (JOSEPH)

"EPHRAIM" (JOSEPH)

River Jordan

GAD

BENJAMIN

(The Philistines) DAN

JERUSALEM

BETHLEHEM

REUBEN

JUDAH (LAND OF JUDEA)

EGYPT

SIMEON

Dead Sea (Salt Sea)

(The Tribe of Levi has no region of its own. Rather, because it is the priestly clan, it possesses cities of its own in every region.)

THE TWELVE TRIBES IN THE LAND OF PROMISE

SIR WYVERN PUGILIST

Author of *Dragon Slayers*

SECRETS of the ANCIENT MANUAL REVEALED!

EVERY DRAGON SLAYER'S GUIDE TO THE BIBLE

PARACLETE PRESS

BREWSTER, MASSACHUSETTS

2015 First Printing
Secrets of the Ancient Manual Revealed! Every Dragon Slayer's Guide to the Bible

Copyright © 2015 by Joyce Denham

ISBN: 978-1-61261-563-9

All quotations from the Bible are paraphrases of Joyce Denham, using the New International Version of the Bible or New Revised Standard Version of the Bible as a starting point.

Library of Congress Cataloging-in-Publication Data

Pugilist, Wyvern, Sir.
  Secrets of the ancient manual revealed! : every dragon slayer's guide to the Bible / Sir Wyvern Pugilist, author of Dragon Slayers.
    pages cm
  Audience: 8-14.
  ISBN 978-1-61261-563-9
  1. Bible—Juvenile literature. 2. Bible stories, English. 3. Sin—Biblical teaching—Juvenile literature. 4. Good and evil—Biblical teaching—Juvenile literature. 5. Satan—Biblical teaching—Juvenile literature. I. Title.
  BS539.P84 2015
  220.6'1—dc23   2015018004

10 9 8 7 6 5 4 3 2 1

Published by Paraclete Press
Brewster, Massachusetts
www.paracletepress.com
Printed in the United States of America

CONTENTS

(Before you read this book)

HOW (ON EARTH) DID WE GET HERE?

Well, before I answer that **REALLY HUGE QUESTION**, let me pose another: Why is our world **SUCH A MESS?!** Forgive my yelling, but someone must state the truth. And the truth is that something has gone terribly wrong in our world. I can tell you right now it has everything to do with vile, despicable, evil, wretched . . . um . . . well, I can only call them "things." I cannot call any one of them "he" or "she" but only "it." There is, however, a name for these "its" and a fitting one: dragons. Our world is inhabited by cruel, unfeeling, icy-blooded **DRAGONS!**

What's that you say? You don't believe in dragons? What?! Okay, let me ask you this: Why do bullies attack kids at your school? Speak, if you know the answer. . . . Very well, I shall tell you: Behind every vicious act of bullying is an outrageously ugly, loathsome (truly disgusting, revolting) dragon called Bucephalus. Or, why do some people not have enough food while others gobble up more than their own body-weights in one meal? Can you tell me? It is obvious: Avarus (how I despise it!) entices the greedy ones. Or, why do people cheat and steal? Do you not know? It's because Youserpin tells them they have every right to take what is not theirs. You see, I could go on and on, but I won't.

Suffice it to say that **DRAGONS EXIST! DRAGONS ARE OUR GREAT UNDOING!** I have met them; I have fought them; I will continue to fight them until the Chief Dragon Slayer commands me to stop.

Whether you believe it or not, we live now in the Land of Dragons.

The beasts have overrun our world, where they scheme and bellow and thrash to the utmost their rot-infested tails. Why? To destroy us, that's why! And to guarantee that we never discover the real truths about the vile reptiles and the means to escape their filthy claws.

Such truths lie hidden in the stories of the *Ancient Manual*.

Lest I've confused you, let me clarify. Folks today have taken to calling the *Ancient Manual* the "Bible." You've heard the word; and you may have been told it is the only name for the Great Book. You and I, however, know the real name of the precious volume, and that is the *only* name I shall use: the *Ancient Manual*. You've also heard, I'm sure, that the stories in the *Ancient Manual* are thousands of years old. They are. Hence the name **ANCIENT** *Manual*.

What's that you say? You tried reading the *Ancient Manual* but you gave up? My friend, you are not alone! The *Ancient Manual* is a most difficult book (although it is, in fact, many, many books, written over a period of 1,500 years, and assembled together in one giant tome). It is filled with antediluvian (prehistoric) mysteries and winding crisscrossing paths leading to dark corners and disguised dragon lairs. Its language is antique (old and musty), its signs and symbols forgotten by superficial modern minds. No wonder so many readers give up on it before they have barely begun.

But giving up is a grave mistake, my friend, a **GRAVE** mistake indeed. Because hidden behind its veils, the *Ancient Manual* holds the world's most valuable treasures: the answers to your questions about dragons. And why they're here. And why we're here with them. It will teach you how to defeat the monsters and how to avoid their foul, reeking breath. What's more, it will reveal much about the Mighty One, who made you and loves you and wants to rescue you from the dragons' snares. Finally, in the *Ancient Manual* you will meet the Chief Dragon Slayer (blessed be His name forever!), who alone possesses the power to free our world from the dragons' icy grip.

As I said, it is a difficult book. Which is why I, Sir Wyvern Pugilist, Slayer of a Thousand and One Dragons (and counting), have written, for your benefit, this modest guide. The importance of my little book is far greater than its size indicates; because through it, I will open for you the locked passageways to the long-hidden chambers of the *Ancient Manual*. I guarantee that once you discover the *Manual's* treasures, you will never be the same. You cannot be. Its riches are too powerful to leave you as you were.

The *Manual* is difficult to read because its language is antique. So, in retelling key stories from the *Manual*, I shall avoid musty language and will present the stories in my own words. Although I shall try to make my own words sound *just a tiny bit like* the antique language of the *Manual*, to give you a sense of what the real thing actually sounds like, and to let you know that the words of the *Manual* are vastly more important than my own, and also because once you've studied the *Manual* as much as I have, its language is stuck in your head and sometimes you just can't get away from it.

What's more, while retelling a story from the *Manual* in a sort of "pretend" *Ancient Manual* voice, I will also give you additional information about the story. I might tell you how it fits with other stories in the *Manual*, and I might point out to you some shocking ideas in the story. At those times I will write in my **OWN VOICE**. That means I shall be flipping back and forth between my "pretend" *Ancient Manual* voice and my ordinary voice. Don't worry, it will all make sense, and you won't get lost.

PLEASE NOTE: I will retell only *a few key stories* from the *Manual*. I will not retell *all* the stories from the Great Book—no, no, no! If I did, this little guidebook would cease to be my little guidebook and would become my enormous guidebook and you would not find the time to read it all the way through. So I shall retell only a small number of stories, stories that enable you to see the bright threads running all the way through the Great Book.

Are the stories I've selected the only ones that reveal the bright threads? **GOOD HEAVENS, NO!** I must begin somewhere, and I have only so much space, and the stories I've selected will suffice to uncover many of the long-hidden secrets of the *Manual*.

FACT: This little book is a **MUST-READ** for every Dragon Slayer that walks the paths of Earth. **DO NOT NEGLECT IT!**

What's that you're asking? "May people who are **NOT** Dragon Slayers read this book?" Well, of course! In fact, they **MUST!** This book is for everyone! But **I WARN YOU:** If you are not yet a Dragon Slayer, but you begin grasping the secrets herein revealed, if you begin walking toward their shining light, I guarantee you will want to become a Dragon Slayer. And you can. Simply study my earlier manual (***Dragon Slayers: The Essential Training Guide for Young Dragon Fighters, Based Wholly on the Practices of the Great Dragon Slayers of Old and the Wisdom of Their* Ancient Manual**) in which you will learn every step to becoming a bona fide Slayer and a member of the Secret Order.

So then, let us all begin our journey to unlock the mysteries of the precious Book. You must summon all your courage and . . . turn . . . the . . . page . . .

NO, WAIT!

STOP!

I forgot the warning.

Do not (I repeat: **DO NOT!**) leave this book unfinished. No, no, no, do not even *think* of committing such a dangerous act! You see, you will surely be tempted to do so, because dragons—especially Cringe Liver, Frantix, and Snuffwick—will whisper in your ears, saying things such as, "Oh my, look, it's raining!" Or, "I wonder what I shall eat today for lunch." Or, "I think I should take a nap right now." Don't you see, the dragons are trying to distract you, drawing your attention away from the *Ancient Manual* to other lesser ideas and activities. Their goal is to ensure you know **NOTHING** about the *Manual*. You might even discover that your copy of this, my little guidebook, has gone missing. But fear not—it is only a nasty trick of a truly stupid dragon. If you do fall prey to their wiles, do not be too hard on yourself. Get up and begin again. By doing so, you will foil the dragons' devious plots.

So, as you read, **BE ON YOUR GUARD!**

DRAGONS ARE EVERYWHERE!

Now, please, turn the page.

NOW!

13

EPEISÓDION ONE

THE AGREEMENT ANTĪQUÁTUS

Let me explain.

The *Ancient Manual* is divided into two parts: Epeisódion One: *The Agreement Antīquátus* (very old and of great use in the distant past, now replaced by something new and better) and Epeisódion Two: *The Agreement Novus Un-Parallelus* (new and without equal). The first Epeisódion is much bigger than the second one. It begins in a time before time, before the world itself even existed. It is there our story begins, in the very first book of the *Ancient Manual*, the book called Genesis, which means (shhhh!) "beginnings."

CHAPTER ONE

A DARK AND TERRIFYING SEA

From THE BOOK CALLED GENESIS

GENESIS

IN THE BEGINNING . . . these are the opening words of the *Ancient Manual*.

In the beginning the Mighty One created the heavens and the **EARTH**. And at first, all was empty and formless, and **DARKNESS** shrouded the uninhabitable **SEA OF CHAOS** where writhing dragons hid themselves in the deeps, hid themselves from the eyes of the Mighty One.

The monsters of the deep dared not catch even a glimpse of the Mighty One's glorious **LIGHT**, the Mighty One's **PERFECT POWER**, the Mighty One's unbounded **GOODNESS**. They despised **GOODNESS**; and because they also despised the Mighty One, they set themselves to blot out the Mighty One's

LIGHT (as if that were even possible!), to dwell in DARKNESS, to break things, to destroy everything that exists. How I despise the beasts!

But the Mighty One, like a great mother bird, hovered over the DARK watery void and SPOKE: "Let there be LIGHT!" And suddenly—LIGHT! The LIGHT banished the DARKNESS to the depths of the old SEA. And the Mighty One BLEW HIS BREATH across the DARK waters; with His BREATH He drove back the SEA OF CHAOS, full of its thrashing dragons, and put strict boundaries around it.

The Mighty One SPOKE AGAIN: "Let there be LAND." And behold—LAND! And the Mighty One SPOKE AGAIN AND AGAIN: "Let there be SUN and MOON and STARS, let there be BIRDS and FISH and CREEPING THINGS that creep on the GROUND, and CATTLE and PLANTS and TREES." And lo!—SUN, MOON, STARS, BIRDS, FISH, CREEPING THINGS that creep on the GROUND, CATTLE, PLANTS, and TREES! Where before there was *nothing*, now there was very much *something*. All because the Mighty One SPOKE, and everything He SPOKE came true. And all of it was GOOD. And the terrifying DARKNESS, banished to the depths of the old SEA, did it no harm.

NOTICE TO READER: Yes, yes, I'm underlining many words. It's because I want you to remember them. When I put words in *italics*, it's for *emphasis* (and I always write *Ancient Manual* in italics, because it is so special). But when I UNDERLINE, it's because I want you to *remember that word* (although you don't need to remember the word UNDERLINE). Why? I'm not telling you—yet.

NOTICE TO READER: Sometimes I refer to the Mighty One (Maker of All That Exists) as "He" (using a capital H), which is not to say that the Mighty One is a man. No, no! The Mighty One is neither a man nor a woman, neither a "he" nor a "she," but is infinitely greater than any "he" or "she." But in speaking of the Mighty One it is sometimes convenient to say "Him" or "He." It means I can avoid repeating "the Mighty One" over and over. So in referring to Him (you see my point), I shall often use "He" or "Him" but always with a capital H. Although the Mighty One is neither a he nor a she, He is, nevertheless, a *person*, which means He is *knowable*. Indeed, He is very knowable and *wants* to be known by *you*, which you will come to understand as you read this book.

After the Mighty One made EARTH and all its CREATURES, He decided to make one more CREATURE, an especially glorious one. (What could it be?) Up until this point, everything on EARTH came into existence—how? Ach, have you forgotten already?! The Mighty One SPOKE it into existence, through His WORD! Ah, but the Mighty One did not (I repeat: **HE DID NOT**) S-P-E-A-K the especially *glorious* CREATURE into existence. Trust me, you'll never guess how He did it, so I'll just tell you: He formed the CREATURE from the GROUND, from EARTH itself. From SOIL! (I told you you'd never guess!) And He named the glorious CREATURE ADAM—which means (you'll never guess this either) "red SOIL." Then the Mighty One BREATHED into ADAM a portion of His own BREATH of LIFE, and He fashioned ADAM in HIS LIKENESS, in HIS OWN IMAGE.

WOW! ADAM bore the IMAGE of the Mighty One! Oh my goodness, do you know what that means? **I DON'T EITHER!** Not completely! But I do know it means that, to some degree, ADAM resembled the Mighty One, could act as His representative, and could WALK AND TALK with Him. They were F-R-I-E-N-D-S. Very GOOD friends.

Then the Mighty One decided to make another glorious creature, to give ADAM a companion. It's true that ADAM was like the Mighty One in some ways; but in others, they greatly differed. Could ADAM create a new world merely by speaking? No. Could ADAM drive back the SEA OF CHAOS with his BREATH? No. Although they were friends, the Mighty One was far, far greater than ADAM. And so, because He loved ADAM and did not want him to be lonely, the Mighty

One decided to take some of the red SOIL from ADAM's body and use it to fashion another CREATURE like ADAM. But the Mighty One would not take *fresh* red SOIL from the EARTH; He would take red SOIL directly from ADAM himself. In that way, the two SOIL-CREATURES (I invented that term) would be made of the very same stuff.

The Mighty One put ADAM into a deep sleep; and while ADAM slept, the Mighty One took a piece of ADAM from the very center of his being and made EVE, which means "mother of all living." So similar were ADAM and EVE that they were like two halves of the same person. ADAM was MALE and EVE was FEMALE, so they fit together perfectly.

The Mighty One BLESSED them, and He commanded them, saying, "Be FRUITFUL and MULTIPLY; FILL the EARTH." By joining their two bodies, ADAM and EVE would create beautiful new SOIL-CREATURES, just like themselves, and those SOIL-CREATURES would also create new SOIL-CREATURES, who would also create new SOIL-CREATURES, and on and on it would go, until the Mighty One's EARTH would be filled with the glorious beings who were His personal friends. And all the SOIL-CREATURES (including *you*) would share the same stuff: the red SOIL from which the Mighty One first made ADAM.

The Mighty One gave ADAM and EVE (and therefore *you, too*) a special job to do: "Take care of EARTH and all its CREATURES," He told them. "Be its protectors."

After six days of creating the world, the Mighty One rested on the SEVENTH (do NOT forget the number seven), making the SEVENTH DAY of every week a day of *rest*.

ADAM loved EVE, just as the Mighty One loved him. And EVE loved ADAM, just as the Mighty One loved her. All day long the two SOIL-CREATURES WALKED AND

TALKED together; but in the evenings when the air was soft and cool they WALKED AND TALKED with the Mighty One, telling Him all about their work. They loved tending the GOOD EARTH because EARTH was in their beings. They were made from it, and for it.

And there was neither DARKNESS nor chaos.

Everything was very, very GOOD, for the whole world was founded on love.

Assignment: (Don't whine—this is extremely important!) Go back through this chapter and make a list of all the UNDERLINED words. Without it, you can *never* unlock the *secrets* of the *Ancient Manual*. DO IT NOW!

HIC
(do not pronounce the "H"!)
SVNT DRACONES

From THE BOOK CALLED GENESIS

GENESIS

I HATE TO TELL YOU THIS NEXT BIT, I really do, because it is heartbreaking. Nevertheless, I must, for I have sworn to tell you the truth. But first . . . **Assignment two:** What's that you're saying? You haven't done the previous assignment? **WHAT?!** Without it, you cannot possibly discover the *Manual's* mysteries! And you can't expect me to do *everything* for you; you must *participate*! Go back to chapter 1 **(DO IT NOW!)** and complete your assignment. I shall wait . . .

Well, I see you're back . . . with your list of *key words* from chapter 1. Phew! Proceed.

Assignment two: Let me explain. The list of words from

chapter 1 is a **SECRET KEY!** The list is a list of *keys* (words) from the **CREATION STORY**, keys that unlock doors—and treasure chests. These *keys* (words) are repeated throughout the *Ancient Manual*, and you must watch for them in the following stories. You'll soon learn that the Mighty One has devised a Grand Plan to *re-create* the Creation, to start it up fresh all over again because of the wretched—oh, sorry—can't tell you that part yet.

But I can tell you that when you find *key words*, you find great treasure, for they stand as beacons of light, giant *hints* declaring that the Mighty One's Grand Plan is *in the works*, it is *moving forward.* It will reveal itself gradually, over a long, long period of time, but when it is finally accomplished there will be a *New* Creation, free of—nope, can't tell you that yet.

SECRET: Very few people know these secret *key words*, so you must *use them well.*

Assignment two: (finally): Keep your list of *key words*

(from chapter 1) close at hand. As you read the following stories, **WATCH** for those *key words* to appear again. Every time you find one, you must either **UNDERLINE** it in your book OR record it and its location (page number) on a separate piece of paper. I'll help you with it at first. By following the *key words*, we'll watch the Grand Plan unfold!

WELL, I've now used up too much space to tell you the story of chapter 2 here in chapter 2. So I shall begin chapter 2 again, on the next page.

SO . . . TURN . . . THE . . . PAGE.

CHAPTER TWO (AGAIN)

HIC
(do not pronounce the "H"!)
SVNT DRACONES
(no, really)

———————

From THE BOOK CALLED GENESIS

GENESIS

AS I WAS SAYING . . . I hate to tell you this, I really do, because it is heartbreaking. But I must, for I have sworn to tell you the truth.

(Begin **ASSIGNMENT TWO** now! And watch for **NEW** *key words* as well. As you read, **ADD THEM** to your list!)

Together with all the **CREATURES** of the **LAND**, **ADAM** and **EVE** lived peacefully (it's true!) in a beautiful **GARDEN** the Mighty One had planted especially for them: the **GARDEN OF DELIGHTS**. Oh, it was Paradise, I tell you, Paradise! Under Adam and Eve's **GOOD** care, the **TREES** grew large, bearing fruit every season. Never did **EARTH** resist their efforts to till its **SOIL**, and never did it refuse to drink its fill of the reliable morning dew. And the **DARK SEA** with dragons hiding in its depths remained far, far, far away, never crossing its boundaries.

Until . . .

It must have occurred while **ADAM** and **EVE** slept. The very **GREATEST** dragon of the deep, that thrashed its tail in vengeance in the watery depths to which the Mighty One had banished it . . . got loose. (Okay, I shall cease underlining—except for adding **NEW** *key words*—and let you carry on the **ASSIGNMENT**, for you are very smart.)

I speak of the **EVIL SEA SERPENT** (add "evil" and "Serpent"), the dragon-of-dragons, the one the other "its" follow and imitate, the one that rides upon their backs, driving them to commit unthinkable iniquities (sins), which is why we in the Secret Order call it the **CHIEF DRAGON RIDER**. It loathes (despises) the Mighty One; it abhors all goodness. And one very dark night, when the moon did not shine, that odious (hateful) Serpent violated its boundaries and crept ever so silently onto the good land. Without uttering a sound, it rose from the depths and crawled upon the wide sands, crawled on its stubby, scaly legs over the rocks, then coiled its long body 'round one of the beautiful trees in the garden and hid itself in the foliage until the morning light.

"Good morning!" the sly Serpent said to Eve as she walked among the trees. "What brings you to this part of the garden so early?"

"Not early at all," said Eve. "It is my regular hour to pick breakfast fruits."

"Try one of these," said the dragon-Serpent, offering her a plump, shiny fruit, hanging from a branch above its head.

"No, no," scolded Eve. "Surely you know: That is the only tree from which the Mighty One forbids us to eat. It will kill us! It contains the knowledge of both good and evil. We already know what is good, but we must never know what is evil, because evil breaks and destroys everything. No, I will not eat from that tree!"

"Oh, Eve, don't be so literal!" the Serpent sneered. "The Mighty One did not mean you will actually die. Did you *not know* that the Mighty One *lies*? He knows that when you eat from this tree you will be wise—as wise as He is! Go ahead then, try it. When you know both good and evil, you will be like God; you will know everything."

Eve thought again.

The Tree of the Knowledge of Good and Evil was beautiful, and its fruit looked scrumptious. If it made her wise, like the Mighty One Himself, then she, too, would be a god. *I would like to be a god*, she thought. She sank her teeth into the fruit. When Adam approached, she offered him a bite. "Eat this, and we will be gods," she said. Then Adam, too, devoured the fruit.

Are you wondering why Eve listened to the vile Serpent? Did she *not know* that the monster was consigned to the deeps? **I DON'T KNOW!** But the **CHIEF DRAGON RIDER** is also the **FATHER OF LIES**. It is **NOT** the Mighty One who lies **(NEVER!)**, but this deplorable dragon-of-dragons. Imagine its camouflage when it spoke to Eve. Why, it glittered with beauty! And its words, so sweet and charming, beguiled her. So lovely did the Serpent appear, Eve did not detect the **DRAGON** behind its disguise.

Upon consuming the horrible fruit, Adam and Eve knew evil: good things broke apart. They looked at each other, and now their nakedness embarrassed them. They ran in opposite directions and hid. In the evening, when He came to walk and talk with them in the cool of the day, the Mighty One called to them:

"Where are you?"

"We are here," whispered Adam. "We hid, because we were naked and ashamed."

"Who told you that you were naked?"

"We ate from the Tree of the Knowledge of Good and Evil, and we saw that we were naked."

"Why did you eat from the tree I warned you against, saying, 'Do not eat from it or you will die'?"

"The Sea Serpent gave the fruit to Eve, and Eve gave the fruit to me," Adam said.

ALERT: I'm about to UNDERLINE again for a *very important* reason. Coming up are even more additional *key words*. You see, what you are reading is what is called the story of "The Fall"—of how the Serpent entered the garden, and DEATH with it, and ruined EVERYTHING. Add these UNDERLINED words to your list, then watch for them to reappear in future stories. They are your keys to the mysteries!

"Oh, Adam," the Mighty One groaned. "Now that you have eaten the toxic fruit, life will be difficult: Earth will oppose you. The ground is CURSED (add it to your list!) because of you; when you till the soil from which you were made, it will be hard as stone, withholding its crops. By SWEAT and TOIL (add these, too) you will grow food. The evil you tasted will break everything."

To Eve the Mighty One said, "You are the Mother of All Living, but the evil you tasted will make becoming a mother PAINful. In hard LABOR and SUFFERING you will deliver your babies. And though you love them, they will not always love you. Some will break your heart."

In burning anger, the Mighty One turned to the wicked Serpent: "CURSED are you! You shall crawl everywhere on your belly and you shall eat dust! Your offspring will be the enemies of Eve's. You will believe you are winning your battles against them, but one day—ONE DAY!—a DESCENDANT (add it!) of Eve will rise to fight you. You will wound his heel, but do not gloat; for he will CRUSH your head!"

Adam and Eve left the Garden of Delights, because evil must not dwell in the garden of goodness. Although they hated what they had done, and they wanted no more of the evil, at the *same time* they *still* desired its deadly fruit. Try as they might, they could not escape the lure of the Serpent's glittering lies. Even when they wanted to choose good, they so often chose evil; and they could not understand why evil had such a grip on them, how it could have invaded them even from the inside, in their hearts.

But that is what evil does.

Two people could not have been more wretched when they departed the Garden of Delights by the EASTern road. (You'll want to remember the word *east*.) The Mighty One placed angels, and a flaming sword that turned in all directions, at the garden's gates, to guard it from any evil thing that might try to enter, and to keep Adam and Eve from *reentering*. "Because," He said, "they might come back to the garden and eat from the Tree of Life, and then they would live forever in their awful state, invaded by evil, under the tyrannical reign of the Chief Dragon Rider (and its awful companion Deathbreath).

IMPORTANT INFORMATION: When the Mighty One speaks, good worlds come into existence. But when the Sea Serpent speaks, everything goes in the opposite direction. Under the spell of the Serpent's lies, the good creation **UNWINDS**. It heads back to the Sea of Chaos. Or maybe I should say the Sea comes roaring onto the land, where it does not belong. However it actually works I'm not sure, but I can tell you truly that the Sea of Chaos and the good land are no longer quite so separated.

Poor Adam and Eve now live outside the Garden of Delights, in a desert of miseries, a place where darkness descends, where pain and tears are common. What's more, the Serpent is there! Did you assume it had slunk back into the Sea? If only! It slithers through lands **EAST** of the garden. And lest you think the revolting monster dozes peacefully behind a rock, think again. I wish that putrid beast *would* sleep, but it is busy—very busy—deceiving the beautiful soil-creatures, sending more and more evil into the world of Adam and Eve's descendants, right down to this present day, right down to this **VERY HOUR!** Always it pollutes our atmosphere with the stink of the old Sea. And that is why bullying goes on in schools, and why some children do not have enough to eat, and why people lie and cheat and steal—because the Serpent convinces them that such things are fine, and that everyone can do exactly as he or she chooses, whenever he or she wants, because (of all the ridiculous things!) he and she believe they are "gods"!

Question: Does the Chief Dragon Rider (the Serpent) act alone?

Answer: Of course not! Hordes of lesser dragons toil under its authority. Once the hideous Rider managed to crawl out of the Sea of Chaos onto the good land, all sorts of other dragons followed it, until the land was **FILLED** with them. That is when the Mighty One's good Earth became the Land of Dragons. The dragons do everything they can to keep us from knowing the Mighty One (who loves us forever) and from reentering the Garden of Delights.

Reader, do you see what has happened? After driving the dragons and their stinking Sea of Chaos far from the good land, the Mighty One commanded the soil-creatures to *fill His Earth*. Immediately, the dragons (the "its" love to reverse the Mighty One's words) seized upon that command and brazenly **FILLED** the Earth with *their own breed!*

MURDER!

From THE BOOK CALLED GENESIS

GENESIS

OUTSIDE THE GARDEN OF DELIGHTS, the slimy Sea Serpent continually tempted Adam and Eve, and they continually swallowed its lies and did its bidding. Despite their fallen state, the Mighty One never stopped loving them, and they clung to the hope that one day—**ONE DAY!**—a man would spring from their descendants to **CRUSH THE SERPENT'S HEAD!**

Meanwhile, the good Creation, so full of riotous life . . . was dying.

Let me explain. There exists a dragon with the power to frighten us beyond belief. No, I speak not of the Chief Dragon Rider—although that Serpent *should* frighten us beyond belief, but we soil-creatures like to pretend it does not exist (it's true, I am not making this up). The dragon I speak of here is Deathbreath (the horror!). It is the Serpent's closest companion and pet. It follows the Serpent EVERYWHERE, because they are joined at the hip. (Yes, yes, I know—serpents don't have hips because they don't have legs. True, very true. But I can see you need to review chapter 2, in which I told you that the Mighty One *cursed* the Serpent, declaring that it would forthwith crawl upon its belly. By which we understand that, until that awful day, the Sea Serpent *did* have legs! So it also had hips, right? I speak now of the Serpent's "hips" merely as vestigial structures—tiny remnants, or leftovers, of what used to exist.) Deathbreath, joined to the old Serpent at its "hip," is a voracious (exceedingly hungry) dragon that eventually swallows every living thing on this broken Earth. Even to think of Deathbreath is to tremble.

That is not to say, however, that after the Serpent's invasion, everything on Earth died at once. Deathbreath works slowly, biding its time, while the Chief Dragon Rider deceives people into believing they will live forever. I'm sorry to say we will not. And that is *exactly* why the Mighty One devised a plan to RESCUE US from both the Chief Dragon Rider (AKA the Sea Serpent) *and* Deathbreath. There would be no point in the Mighty One rescuing His Creation from only one or the other, because, as I said, they work together. The Grand Plan of Rescue began when the Mighty One first warned the Serpent that one day—ONE DAY!—a descendant of Eve will arrive to CRUSH the monster's head. And I can tell you right now that when the Serpent's head is CRUSHED, Deathbreath will die! That's right: Deathbreath will DIE! Earth will be reborn. Ah, but I am getting ahead of the story. For now, we must go back to Adam and Eve in their new life outside the Garden of Delights.

Because she was **NAKED**, Eve did not want Adam to look upon her; and because he was **NAKED**, Adam did not want Eve to look upon him. Whereas before they felt no shame in seeing each other exactly as they were, now they disliked who they were, and neither one wanted the other to look too closely. They sewed leaves together—to cover themselves.

When the Mighty One saw how they suffered, His heart ached. His soil-creatures no longer acted like the two halves of one person. Although they longed for each other, they felt far apart. They argued; they wept; they blamed each other. And when the Mighty One called, they seldom recognized His voice. They feared He hated them and refused to speak (this fear was one of the Serpent's ugly lies); so they hid—from the Mighty One, and from each other.

The Mighty One took the skins of animals and made clothes for Adam and Eve to cover their nakedness. It meant that some animals died. (Where else would the hides have come from?) And when things died, the Mighty One groaned, because Deathbreath did not belong (no it did **NOT**) in the good world the Mighty One had made.

Question: Why didn't the Mighty One simply destroy the Serpent and Deathbreath?

Answer: Oh, my friend, it is not that simple! You see, the Serpent's evil had entwined itself all 'round the Soil-Creatures' hearts. Destroying the evil would mean destroying the Soil-Creatures as well. And the Mighty One will not (He **WILL NOT**) do so, because he *loves* us.

Adam worked hard to till the stone-hard Earth. And Eve labored in pain to bring their children into the world. Their first child, a son, they named Cain. Eve bore a second son and they named him Abel. Cain became a farmer, and Abel became a shepherd. Time passed, and one day Cain brought fruits from his farm and offered them to the Mighty One on an altar. (An offering is a ritual in which a person takes from the very best he or she owns, holds it up, and gives it to the Mighty One. It's a special way to thank the Mighty One for all that He gives us, including our very lives.) The best fruits are always the first fruits of the crop, but Cain did not offer those; he brought the fruits he didn't want. Abel brought lambs from his herds and offered them to the Mighty One. The first-born lambs are always the most valuable, and those are what he offered. He knew that all things come from the Mighty One and he trusted the Mighty One to take care of him, so he did not fear giving up the lambs. The Mighty One accepted Abel's offering of thanksgiving, but He did not accept Cain's, for very little thanksgiving was in it.

Cain's anger boiled.

"Why are you angry?" the Mighty One asked. "If you do what is right, you too will be accepted. But if you listen to the Serpent's lies and serve only yourself, then watch out—evil lurks at your door like a wild animal waiting to rip you apart. You must say no to it."

"Come into the field with me," Cain said to Abel. So Abel went into the field with him, and Cain rose up against Abel and **MURDERED** him. It was then that Eve experienced a pain beyond the pain of giving birth, a pain that never goes away: Her firstborn son had broken her heart.

The Mighty One called to Cain: "Where is your brother, Abel?"

Cain said, "How should I know? Am I my brother's personal protector?"

WARNING: Cover your ears, this will be loud. **"YES, CAIN! YOU ARE YOUR BROTHER'S PERSONAL PROTECTOR!!"** Oh, reader, did not the Mighty One charge Adam and Eve, and their descendants, including *us*, with safeguarding the Creation? Abel is part of the Creation, so Cain—**HIS OWN BROTHER!**—should have watched over him! Instead, he killed him. It was the world's *first murder*, brother killing brother.

The Mighty One said, "Cain, what have you done? Listen! Do you not hear those agonizing wails? It is your brother's blood crying to me from the ground. *Cursed* are you from the ground, the ground that swallowed Abel's blood! When you till the soil, it will yield no crops. You must leave your farm and wander Earth as an exile."

Oh . . . my . . . goodness! Do these words not remind you of the Mighty One's words after Adam and Eve ate the awful fruit? The Mighty One cursed *not* Adam and Eve but the evil Serpent and the ground. Now Cain, too, is cursed, cursed *from* the ground—in other words, he cannot till the ground at all. If he plants seeds, they will not sprout. Earth will not share its life with him. Just as his parents left the Garden of Delights, he will leave his farm and wander Earth, a murderous soil-creature miserably estranged (separated, with no feelings of affection) from the soil itself.

"No!" whined Cain. "My punishment is too great! Not only will I be driven from the fields, I will be driven from You, O Creator! And when I wander Earth, someone might kill me!" (Oh, **PULEEZE!**)

"No," said the Mighty One. "I will put a mark on you, Cain, so no one will harm you." Cain left the presence of the Mighty One. (Ach! I cannot *imagine* living outside the presence of the Mighty One!) He wandered in the Land of Nod (it means "Land of Wandering"), where he could not hear the Mighty

One's voice; he wandered far *east* of the Garden of Delights, much farther than his parents had ever traveled.

NOTE: Did you observe that the only time Abel speaks in this story is after he's dead? His *blood* speaks from the ground. Later in the *Ancient Manual* we're told that "the life of the flesh is in the blood." When Cain spilled Abel's blood, he spilled Abel's life. Cain sided with Deathbreath! But the Mighty One heard Abel's blood, heard it crying from the ground. Truly, He hears it to this very day. And one day—**ONE DAY!**—the special descendant of Eve will appear to avenge Abel's murder. He will defeat Deathbreath and raise Abel's life from the soil. He will remake Abel, and Abel will **LIVE!**

Did you notice (well, you couldn't miss it, could you?) that though Cain viciously murdered Abel, and though Cain was cursed from the ground, his life was spared? Ah, now you begin to see how much the Mighty One loves everything He's made—even Cain. Perhaps Cain will someday change his mind and follow the Mighty One's good ways of love and faithfulness. If Cain *does* choose the Mighty One's ways, what do you think the Mighty One will do? You are right—He will remake Cain into a new person, freed from his bondage to the Serpent.

(I hope you watched for *key words* in this chapter. You did **NOT?!** Read through it again—**DO IT NOW!**—and underline or record the words on your list. I cannot tell you how important it is to continue **ASSIGNMENT TWO** all the way through this book!)

CHAPTER FOUR

THE MAN
WHO DIDN'T DIE

From THE BOOK CALLED GENESIS

GENESIS

THE MIGHTY ONE **BLESSED** ADAM AND EVE with many more children, beginning with a son named Seth, who was like his slain brother Abel. And the Mighty One **BLESSED** all the children with more children, and He **BLESSED** those children with more children; the beautiful **SOIL-CREATURES** were **FRUITFUL** and had **MULTIPLIED** so many times over, they **FILLED** the **EARTH** with people much like their first ancestors, **ADAM** and **EVE**. Despite being driven from the **GARDEN OF DELIGHTS**, and despite all the death that had entered the world, the <u>**SOIL-CREATURES**</u> fulfilled the Mighty One's command: <u>*BE FRUITFUL AND MULTIPLY; FILL THE EARTH*</u>. (Yes, I've been underlining, to remind you to watch for *key words*. Now you do it.)

WARNING: This next bit might be boring—because it's another list. But lists can be very important, and this particular list is **EXTREMELY IMPORTANT!** It is a *genealogy* of the early descendants of Adam and Eve. **PAY ATTENTION!**

THE GENEALOGY OF ADAM AND EVE'S SONS

- When Adam and Eve had lived many, many years, they became the parents of a son in their image, in their own likeness; they named him Seth.
- After Seth was born, Adam lived hundreds of years more, and he had many more sons and daughters—and he died.

  Oh, no! Adam (and Eve) **DIED!** (See what you can learn from a list?)
- Seth became the father of Enosh, and Seth lived hundreds of years more, and he had many more sons and daughters—and he died.
- Enosh became the father of Kenan, and Enosh lived hundreds of years more, and he had many more sons and daughters—and he died.
- And Kenan became the father of Mahalalel, and Kenan lived hundreds of years more, and he had many more sons and daughters—and he died.

  (It's an awful *pattern*: Everyone has children and then *dies*! **CURSE THAT ROTTEN DEATHBREATH!**)
- And Mahalalel became the father of Jared, and Mahalalel lived hundreds of years more, and he had many more sons and daughters—and he died.
- And Jared became the father of Enoch, and Jared lived hundreds of years more, and he had many more sons and daughters—and he died.
- And Enoch became the father of Methuselah, and Enoch (reader, **WATCH**

CAREFULLY) *walked with the Mighty One for hundreds of years*, and he had many more sons and daughters (WATCH CAREFULLY) and Enoch *kept walking with the Mighty One, and then he was* NO MORE, *because the Mighty One* TOOK HIM.

WHAT?! What does this mean, "the Mighty One *took* him"? It means that Enoch did not die (I repeat: ENOCH DID NOT DIE!!). It means the Mighty One snatched him away into the Mighty One's unseen realm. Enoch escaped Deathbreath! Enoch's story is how things were meant to be from *the beginning* (as in, the Creation story). *In the beginning*, soil-creatures walked and talked with the Mighty One . . . and . . . they . . . did . . . not . . . die. That's how it was *supposed* to be. Until the Sea Serpent slithered into the Garden. Well, up until this point in the story, I don't think anyone had walked with the Mighty One quite as closely as Enoch.

It's exciting, I admit, this story about Enoch escaping Deathbreath. But there's even more to it.

Question: Is Enoch a descendant of Adam and Eve?

Answer: Yes! We can see that in the genealogy (lists can be so important). You can trace his ancestry straight back to both of them. It's a clue—of what's to come. When the Mighty One cursed the slimy Serpent, He told that Father of Lies that one day—ONE DAY!—a descendant of Eve would arrive to CRUSH the Serpent's head, which also means the end of Deathbreath, because Death-breath is the Serpent's companion—they ALWAYS go together.

Well then, here's Enoch—a descendant of Eve—and the bilious (look it up!) Deathbreath has no power over him. Is Enoch the promised descendant who will crush the Serpent's ugly head, rendering Deathbreath powerless too? We don't know yet. Resume reading the genealogy:

- And Methuselah became the father of Lamech, and Methuselah lived hundreds of years more, and he had many more sons and daughters—and he died. (I repeat: he **DIED!**) Pardon my yelling—it's just that Methuselah, Enoch's son, **DIED!** Oh, it is so horrible! Only Enoch escaped the bilious (did you look it up?) Deathbreath's squeezing clutches. Everyone else keeps dying. So I guess Enoch is *not* the special descendant of Eve, the one who will one day—**ONE DAY!**—utterly defeat the Serpent *and* Deathbreath. We must keep watching. (And, sadly, we must finish the list.)

- And Lamech became the father of a son **(WATCH CAREFULLY)**, and he named his son Noah, saying, "From out of the ground that the Mighty One cursed, when He also cursed the Serpent, Noah shall bring us relief from the difficult toil with which we must now till the soil." (Aha! Another descendant of Eve has arrived. And did you notice the abundance of *key words*—the ones you've been listing—in this paragraph?) Do you know what the name Noah means? It means "rest." Recall that after the Mighty One spent *six days* creating the world, on the *seventh day* He *rested*. And He commanded all soil-creatures to do the same: Rest on the seventh day.

But since the Serpent first deceived them, the soil-creatures have hardly rested at all. The cursed ground refuses to readily provide crops, and so the soil-creatures work very hard to grow food.

Hope comes with the birth of Noah, whose name means *rest*. Oh, I can hear what you're asking: "But how? How will Noah bring relief from the exhausting toil?" Well, give me a minute, will you? Have patience, and *keep reading!* We must finish the genealogy:

- And Lamech lived hundreds of years more, and he had many more sons and daughters—and he died.

- And Noah became the father of three sons: Shem, Ham (it does *not* mean roast pig), and Japheth.

  So ends the list of Adam and Eve's early descendants.

IMPORTANT INFORMATION:

1. Through Enoch, we learn that Deathbreath does *not* have the final word! Soil-creatures, even though they die, can live! (More on this later.)

2. Alas, Enoch is *not* the descendant of Eve who will one day arrive to crush the Serpent's head, but he *foreshadows* him. (A *foreshadowing* is a sign of something that will happen in the future. When Enoch escapes death, it is a signal to the world that one day someone else will arrive, someone like Enoch, who will *defeat* and *destroy* Deathbreath forever.)

3. Through Noah, we learn that the Mighty One's curse on the ground—that turned the Earth dry and unyielding—can be reversed. With Noah comes the hope of *rest*, rest from the bondage of endless toil, rest such as Adam and Eve once enjoyed in the Garden of Delights.

What on Earth is Noah about to do?

GENEOLOGY LEADING TO THE SPECIAL DESCENDANT OF EVE:

ADAM & EVE *to* ABRAHAM & SARAH

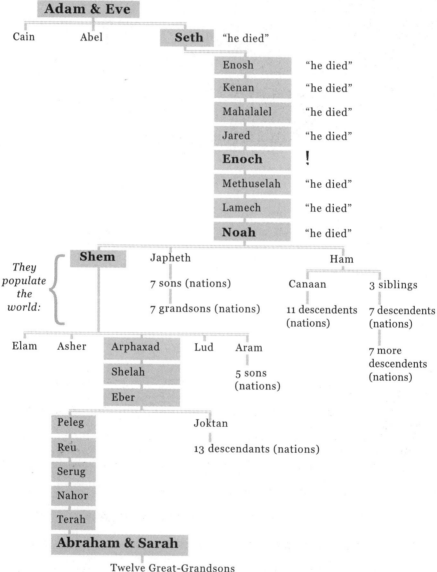

Adam & Eve

Cain   Abel   **Seth**   "he died"

Enosh   "he died"

Kenan   "he died"

Mahalalel   "he died"

Jared   "he died"

Enoch   !

Methuselah   "he died"

Lamech   "he died"

Noah   "he died"

They populate the world: **Shem**   Japheth   Ham

7 sons (nations)   Canaan   3 siblings

7 grandsons (nations)   11 descendents (nations)   7 descendents (nations)

Elam   Asher   Arphaxad   Lud   Aram   7 more descendents (nations)

Shelah   5 sons (nations)

Eber

Peleg   Joktan

Reu   13 descendants (nations)

Serug

Nahor

Terah

Abraham & Sarah

Twelve Great-Grandsons

(Geneology continues on p. 123)

CHAPTER FIVE

THE GREAT RESCUE

From THE BOOK CALLED GENESIS

GENESIS

WHEN THE SOIL-CREATURES MULTIPLIED upon the face of the ground, the Mighty One said, "My breath shall not remain in the soil-creatures forever, for they are flesh. Their years shall now be only one hundred and twenty." (Aha!—*key words* from the Creation story: *soil-creatures, multiplied, ground, breath*. I'm sure you noticed them. Puleeze continue **ASSIGNMENT TWO!**)

And the Mighty One saw that the wickedness of the soil-creatures was great, spreading across the face of the Earth. Even when they wanted to do good, they often did evil. The Serpent's stinking lies took root in their hearts and minds; they became self-centered and full of hate: They became DRAGON RIDERS! Living in such a broken condition, no wonder the inclinations and thoughts of the soil-creatures' hearts were continually evil. Earth was in ruins. (Yes, more key words: *soil-creatures, Earth, good, evil, Serpent*.)

So the Mighty One, who so loved His world, nevertheless was *sorry* He had put the soil-creatures on Earth.

STOP! That word *sorry*—it means something much greater than "Oh, sorry about that." If we were reading this section of the *Ancient Manual* in its most ancient language (ancient Hebrew)—which we cannot, of course, because I myself am not fluent in ancient Hebrew, nor are you—we would discover (thanks to my extensive research into the meanings of ancient Hebrew words) that the word *sorry* actually means . . . you'll hardly believe this, but it's true . . . it means . . . to expel a whole lot of BREATH! It means to GREATLY SIGH. In other words, the Mighty One is not just *sorry* (as we would use the word today)—He is heaving a giant SIGH of remorse.

Question: Does not the Mighty One's *breath* of sorrow appear in striking contrast to the Mighty One's *breath* that blew across the face of the dark waters in the opening lines of the Creation story?

Answer: Yes! It also appears in striking contrast to the Mighty One's *breath* that He *breathed* into Adam. In those prehistoric moments, the Mighty One *breathed life* into His Creation. But now, after the Serpent took up residence on Earth, the Mighty One *breathes* a sigh of great sadness.

So the Mighty One said, "I will wipe away from Earth the soil-creatures I have made, along with cattle, and creeping things that creep on the ground, and birds of the air, and trees and plants, for I sigh deeply over them."

But Noah found grace (unearned favor and mercy) in the eyes of the Mighty One.

Earth was dying—it was filled with violence. How different from *the beginning*, when Earth was filled with living things. *In the beginning* the Mighty One saw that Earth was *good*; now He saw that it was decaying, for all flesh had corrupted its behavior on Earth. The Mighty One said to Noah, "I have decided to end all flesh, because Earth is filled with the violence of the soil-creatures. Make yourself an ark." (An ark is a treasure chest, or—in this case—a floating one, a boat. But how very odd! Why should Noah make a boat, if everything is going to be destroyed?) "Build the ark of cypress wood and cover it with tar inside and out. Put a window in it . . ." (Oh my goodness! In ancient Hebrew that word *window* means "light"! Recall the Mighty One's first command to the Creation: "Let there be light!" Now He commands light to shine into the *ark*. Is the ark *the beginning* of a *New* Creation?) "Put a door in the ark; and build three decks inside. That is your part to do, Noah. For my part, I will send a flood of waters to cover my Earth."

These waters can only be the ancient Sea of Chaos! The Mighty One will strip off the boundaries He placed around it, permitting the awful Sea to flood back in! "The waters will destroy all flesh that carries the breath of life. All creatures on Earth will die—but not you, Noah, neither you nor your wife, nor your sons, nor your sons' wives, for all of you will enter the ark, and there I will keep you alive. You shall bring two of every living thing into the ark with you. Bring them in twos, male and female, of all birds, all cattle, and all things that creep upon the ground—bring seven pairs of every single kind—to keep them alive. Take also every sort of food into the ark with you, so that you and all the animals will have plenty to eat."

Why, it's almost comical, isn't it?—the way the Mighty One says, "I'm going to destroy everything" and then proceeds to SAVE EVERYTHING by rescuing *seven pairs*, *male* and *female*, of every kind, meaning that every kind of creature will produce offspring, *multiplying* itself all over again. You can see that, even though this is the story of the destroying flood, it is also the story of the GREAT RESCUE. In fact—and this is truly amazing!—in the Great Rescue, the Mighty One begins *the beginning* all over again! He will make a new Creation from the seeds of the original one, the seeds stored in His treasure chest—the ark.

Noah did everything the Mighty One commanded him.

Oh, how very different he is from Adam and Eve, who were given only one command: Do not eat from the Tree of the Knowledge of Good and Evil. Only one command, but they didn't keep it. Noah is given many commands, and he keeps each and every one.

ALERT: Note the plethora (loads) of *key words* throughout this chapter. They're EVERYWHERE—so much so, it's like reading the Creation story all over again. I can barely resist underlining them myself, but I won't spoil your excitement in discovering them.

Then the Mighty One said to Noah, "Go into the ark, you and all your family, for I have witnessed that, of all the soil-creatures now living on Earth, you alone do what is right. Take with you seven pairs of every kind of bird and animal, to keep them alive on the face of the Earth. Because in seven days—" (SEVEN DAYS—the same number of days in the original Creation story) "in *seven days*, I will send rain upon the Earth for FORTY days and FORTY nights."

STOP! PULEEZE remember that number *forty*: Add it to your list of *key words.* Do it **NOW!**

The Mighty One continued: "And every living thing I have made will be wiped from the face of the ground."

Noah did all that the Mighty One commanded him.

Do you see what's happening?! The original Creation story is running in **REVERSE**! After *seven days*, the *Sea of Chaos* will *return*, covering the Earth with the waters of the deep, blotting out *all created life.* Creation is going to **UNWIND**.

During those *seven days*, the Mighty One will *begin creating* Earth all over again—from the seeds of the first Earth. The Mighty One saves *seven* breeding pairs of every kind of bird and animal. He saves many pairs of soil-creatures— Noah and his wife, Shem and his wife, Ham and his wife, and Japheth and his wife. It's like having four "Adams and Eves" with which to begin the second Creation!

Noah's family, together with seven pairs of every kind of bird and animal and every creeping thing that creeps on the ground, went into the treasure chest—the ark—and the Mighty One **SHUT THE DOOR** behind them, to safeguard them from the waters of Chaos. After seven days the dark waters flooded the old Earth. The fountains of the deep burst forth. The windows of the heavens opened, and it rained for **FORTY** days and nights.

Everything on the face of the old Earth died. But Noah and his wife, and their sons and their sons' wives, and all the living creatures in the ark, seven pairs of each, male and female, the Mighty One saved alive.

The Mighty One remembered Noah (whose name means what?) and all the creatures with him in the ark, and the Mighty One caused a great wind to blow over the waters. (Did you get that? That's exactly how the original Creation began! This one begins in the *same way*.)

The breath of the Mighty One blew over the dark waters, and the dark waters retreated. After many, many days, Noah looked out the window in the ark, and he saw that the ground was dry. The Mighty One opened His treasure chest and said to Noah, "Go forth from the ark, you and your wife, and your sons and your sons' wives, and all the living creatures that are in the ark with you—every kind of bird and cattle and all the creeping things that creep on the ground. And the Mighty One *blessed* Noah and his family, and all the creatures, and said to them: "Be *fruitful* and *multiply* and *fill* the Earth!"

They did. The four new "Adams and Eves"—and all the birds and cattle and creeping things, male and female—produced offspring; and those offspring produced offspring; and those produced offspring, and on and on it went until the Earth was once again filled with birds and cattle and creeping things and beautiful soil-creatures. In this way, Noah, because he obeyed the Mighty One's good commands, brought hope and rest to the damaged Creation.

When Noah emerged from the ark, he built an altar, and he and everyone in his family bowed in worship to the Mighty One, and everything seemed so very good.

ALERT: I shall now begin to (occasionally) add references to the margins of this book. What are references? They name the chapters and verses in the *Ancient Manual* (aka the Bible) where you can find the story or the lines I am quoting from the Great Book. References are often of special interest to the adults looking over a Dragon Slayer's shoulder while he or she is studying this, my most excellent guide to the *Ancient Manual*. Trust me, adults can't wait to get their hands on Dragon Slayer books! (Politely suggest that they purchase their own copies.) Now, getting back to the story of Noah . . .

And when the Mighty One smelled the pleasing odor of the smoke from the altar, He said, "Never again will I curse the ground because of the soil-creatures, for the inclinations of their hearts are evil continually; and never again will I destroy my Earth with a flood. As long as Earth endures, seedtime and harvest, summer and winter, day and night shall not cease." And the Mighty One placed a rainbow (a **RAINBOW!**) in the sky as a sign that He will never again destroy Earth with a flood.

* GENESIS 8:21

GENESIS 9:8-17

GENESIS 9:5-6

The Mighty One gave Noah and his family, and all the new soil-creatures that came from them, a Law: No murder. **NO MURDER!** If they could follow this one Law, perhaps Earth would remain free from violence.

So the Mighty One began the Creation all over again, and all the violence was gone. (That's very good.) He remade the Earth from its seeds. Everything was new. (That's fantastic!) Obviously, I'm breathing a huge sigh of relief. But—oh dear—the inclinations of the soil-creatures hearts are still **EVIL CONTINUALLY!** That means that, even though Creation enjoys a new *beginning*, and the awful Sea is pushed back, the evil Sea Serpent is **STILL HERE**. It still **LIES** and deceives us, still sends **DEATHBREATH** to destroy life! And if the Serpent and Deathbreath remain, that means their lesser dragon-servants also remain. Why were these creeps not wiped out in the flood? **I DON'T KNOW**. But remember—they can swim.

Question: Was Noah a descendant of Eve?

Answer: Yes.

* This is your first reference: It contains the name of the book in the *Ancient Manual*, followed by the number of the chapter in that book, followed by the number/s of the verse/s. This particular reference tells you that I am now quoting a line from the book called Genesis, chapter 8, verse 21.

Question: Was Noah the special descendant of Eve who will one day—**ONE DAY!**—arrive to forever free the world from the Serpent and Deathbreath, and all lesser dragons?

Answer: No. But Noah *foreshadows* him, because Noah loved and followed the Mighty One; and he said no to the Serpent; and his name means *rest*. He is a sign of the special descendant to come.

CHAPTER SIX

THE TOWER OF
BABY TALK

From THE BOOK CALLED GENESIS

WARNING: If you don't keep track of the *key words* on your list, you'll get lost and fail to unlock the secrets in the *Ancient Manual*.

GENESIS

VENTUALLY THE FLOODING SEA WATERS abated (decreased) and Earth was dry. Noah's sons and their wives were fruitful and multiplied, and from their descendants came many, many nations, and all the nations spoke only one language. (Yes, yes, I saw them too—*Sea, Earth, fruitful, multiplied, descendants.*)

They migrated *west* (are they heading back toward the old Garden of Delights, perhaps looking for it?) and settled on a great plain, and there they said to one another, "Enough of this nomadic life, following our herds, moving with the seasons! Let's settle in one place. We can make bricks and mortar. We can build a city! In the city wall, we can build a tower so high, it will reach to the heavens—where the gods dwell. If we reach the gods, nothing can stop us. We will be great and powerful; we, too, will be gods!"

Sound familiar? Is this not the **SAME LIE** the Serpent spoke to Eve? "You will be gods!" Ha! It's the same-old, same-old. The Serpent's lies never change. Oh yes, it dresses them up to attract people in various times and places, but underneath, at their core, they are the same disgusting, **DEATH-INDUCING LIES!** They are designed to keep us from ever knowing the Mighty One who loves us so much . . . well, I cannot describe how much He loves us.

My dear reader, despite the Great Rescue when the Creation began afresh, the Serpent, and Deathbreath, and all the lesser dragons, too, remained in our world, and once again evil grew, and grew, and grew.

Did you notice that the soil-creatures no longer even *mention* the Mighty One? They speak only of "the heavens"—where they believe "gods," or nature spirits, dwell. These so-called gods never lower themselves to visit creatures on Earth. They are too high, too above-it-all. So the soil-creatures decided to climb up to the gods. Did you get that?! They tried to **CLIMB** to the gods! Why, who would do such a thing?! Especially after seeing in the Creation story that the One True God—the Mighty One—has already *come down* to us! Remember how He walked and talked with Adam and Eve in the Garden of Delights? We don't need to climb high towers to find the Mighty One. In fact, we cannot. How could we ever climb high enough to reach the Creator of the Universe? The good news is that *He* has come down to *us*.

But the soil-creatures remember nothing about the Mighty One—nothing. They sense a power greater than their own, an unseen power that dwells beyond their world, but they have no idea what (or who) it is. They look at the beautiful Creation surrounding them, and as they do, the dragons whisper into their hearts and minds, saying, "Look at the sun, moon, and stars, the clouds, the rivers, the trees and rocks, the birds of the air, the cattle, and all the creeping things that creep on the ground—these are your gods. They control Earth and they control you. Do not make them angry, or they will harm you."

Why, I never . . . ! Such a stinking lie! So great was the lie, the soil-creatures swallowed it whole, although I'm surprised they didn't choke. They made statues of the "gods" they believed inhabited the rocks and trees, the rivers, clouds, sun, moon, stars, the cattle, and all the creeping things that creep on the ground. They bowed down to them, worshiping the Creation rather than the good Creator. They did everything they could to make their so-called gods hear them. They even . . . oh, this is so evil, I can barely speak of it . . . but I must tell you the truth about the world, about some things that happened thousands of years ago. These early soil-creatures sacrificed some of their children—**THEIR OWN CHILDREN!**—to the so-called gods. Of course, the "gods" could hear or see nothing, for they were only wood and stone images of the beautiful things the Mighty One had made.

Not only that, the soil-creatures wanted to become gods. That is why they built the high tower, to lift them to the highest gods of the heavens, so they could talk to the gods and persuade the gods to help them and turn *them* into gods too. They also believed their high tower would make them famous.

LEVITICUS 18:21;
JEREMIAH 32:35

"Ha-ha!" they laughed. "When other soil-creatures see how great we are, they will want to worship us. No one will be more famous, more powerful, more popular than **WE!** It's all about **WEEEEE!**—no, it's all about **US!**—or is it **WE?**—no, it must be **US!**—"

Well, they were so arrogant, and so dull, they could not recognize their grave mistakes, couldn't even remember when to use "we" and when to use "us" in a proper sentence. So the Mighty One decided something must be done about their language. If they continued to all speak the same language, there would be **NO END** to their pride! Just think of how many towers they might build to the gods. Those towers would lift their pride to such heights, even if the Mighty One **SHOUTED** to them they would no longer hear Him **AT ALL!**

"I shall confuse their language," said the Mighty One. "Otherwise, no evil will be impossible for them." So the Mighty One went down to Earth— although they could not see Him—and He confused their language. Suddenly, they could not understand each other. When one friend spoke to another, they each heard only gibberish—baby talk. "Stop babbling like a baby!" one brother said to his sister. And his sister, who understood not one word of what he said to her, said to him, "Stop babbling like a baby!"

It was hopeless to go on building the tower. No one could understand anyone else, so no one was in charge.

That is when the Mighty One scattered the soil-creatures across Earth. Bit by bit, each group began to understand its own members, and soon the world was filled with many, many languages. No longer could all the soil-creatures on Earth act together to fulfill their arrogant dreams of climbing to the gods and becoming gods themselves. Now they were divided, living in different parts of the world. Those divisions protected them, to some degree, from the greatest lies of the Serpent. It kept their immeasurable pride from growing SO IMMENSE they might destroy each other altogether.

So the tall tower was never finished. To this very day it stands in ruins and everyone calls it the Tower of Babel—the Tower of Baby Talk.

It would be a long time indeed before the divided soil-creatures might once again attempt to understand each other, and help each other, and, maybe, even begin to love each other. It would be a long time indeed before they listened once again to the calls of the Mighty One.

CHAPTER SEVEN

A PROMISE KEPT

From THE BOOK CALLED GENESIS

GENESIS

A LONG, LONG TIME AFTER the Tower of Baby Talk, and approximately four thousand years ago today, there lived in the City of Ur (just say "Errrr") a man named Abraham and his wife, Sarah. Abraham was a descendant of Noah, who was a descendant of Enoch, who was a descendant of Seth, who was a son of Adam and Eve.

(Abraham is a descendant of Eve! Could he be the descendant who will one day—**ONE DAY!**—arrive to **CRUSH** the Serpent's head?)

Abraham and Sarah were wealthy. They lived in an important city; they had clothes, and food, and gold, and pots and pans, and other stuff. The only thing they lacked was a child.

FACT: In Abraham's day, a man's most valuable possessions were (1) an inheritance from his father; and (2) a son, through whom his line of descendants could live on. The fact that Abraham and Sarah had no son was a **HUGE** problem and a **GREAT** shame to them.

FACT: In the ancient world, a woman's greatest honor was being a mother.

Just like everyone else, Abraham and Sarah worshiped little statues of wood or stone, their so-called "gods." They knew nothing about the Mighty One, Maker of Heaven and Earth.

One day, the Mighty One **SPOKE** to Abraham. I believe He spoke *out loud*! He said, "Abraham, leave Ur, your great city, and go to a land I will show you. If you follow me to that land, I will make you fruitful; you will multiply, and I will make from your children a great nation. I will bless you. I will make your name great and you will be a blessing to all the nations on Earth."

I'm so excited! Did you notice lots of *key words* from the original Creation story? You did **NOT**?! Then **STOP READING!** Go back right now and review your list! I'll wait . . .

Okay, I see you're back. Yes, the words are *descendant, spoke, land, fruitful, multiply, bless, blessing, Earth.* Here we go again: it sounds like the Creation story, doesn't it? Exactly! From here forward, you must pay special attention to the word **LAND**. **LAND** is so important: the Mighty One created it for our safe and secure habitation. When He finally makes the *New* Creation, it will be all about **LAND**. The word **LAND** is a marvelous clue provided by the *key words*: it tells us that the Grand Plan to re-create **EARTH** is happening; the Mighty One is preparing **LAND** for Abraham and Sarah, just as He once prepared **GOOD**, safe **LAND** for Adam and Eve.

GENESIS 12:1-3;
GENESIS 15:1-6;
GENESIS 17:1-8

Abraham heard the Mighty One's voice (he heard it, he heard it!), and he answered. He and Sarah left Ur, living in tents again, like nomads, not knowing where they were going, until the Mighty One guided them to the **LAND** of Promise. At that time, the wicked Canaanites (scary, violent people) lived in that land. But the Mighty One appeared to Abraham—(**STOP RIGHT THERE!** Did you get that? The Mighty One *appeared* to Abraham! Wow!)— and said to him, "To your **DESCENDANTS** I will give all this **LAND**."

Abraham answered, "O Mighty One, I have no descendants."

When it was dark, the Mighty One led Abraham outside the door of his tent to look at the sky. He said, "Count the stars, Abraham." Abraham said, "I cannot, for there are too many to count." The Mighty One said, "That will be the number of your descendants—too many to count."

Abraham believed the Mighty One's Word. And the Mighty One observed that Abraham trusted Him. He thought, *Abraham is a righteous man, because he believes my Word.* Then the Mighty One swore, in an eternally binding covenant (a forever agreement) with Abraham, that He, the Mighty One, would fulfill his two great promises to Abraham: to give him **LAND** and **DESCENDANTS**. Abraham and Sarah would be *fruitful* and *multiply*, in their own *land*.

But when Abraham was ninety-nine years old, he still had no child. Then the Mighty One appeared (!) to Abraham again and said, "I am God Almighty, walk before me in blamelessness."

Oh . . . my . . . goodness! Not only has the Mighty One *appeared* to Abraham—**TWICE!**—He tells Abraham to *walk* with Him—just as Adam and Eve walked with Him in the Garden of Delights!

Abraham fell to his face, and the Mighty One said, "I will keep my promise, Abraham: You shall become the father of many, many nations, and I will give to your descendants the Land of Promise. Your wife, Sarah, shall have a son. Nations and kings shall come from her. Call your son Isaac."

STOP! Abraham and Sarah remind us of Adam and Eve, don't they? They are a married couple and they are given special land the Mighty One prepares for them. Now try thinking of their old city, Ur (it was a wicked city), as if it's the old *Sea of Chaos*. (You say you cannot?! Oh, **PULEEZE!** Use your imagination!) They must leave Ur (the "Sea"), because the Mighty One has driven back the Sea and made good land for all His beautiful creatures.

USEFUL SUMMARY: The Creator told Adam and Eve to be fruitful and multiply, and they did, but their descendants committed great violence on Earth, and so they all died when the Sea flooded back in—except for Noah and his family. The Mighty One rescued Noah's family; and they acted like new "Adams" and "Eves," multiplying, filling the Earth. But their descendants also did evil, because the Serpent and Deathbreath and all the lesser dragons did not die in the flood. Now we've come to Abraham and Sarah. Amazingly, the Mighty One *appears* to them, walks and talks with them, just as He did with Adam and Eve. And Sarah, like Eve, will have a son, from whom many, many descendants will be born—many, many nations of soil-creatures. (I do hope you found all the *key words* above.)

Question: Will Sarah's son be the special descendant of Eve who will one day—**ONE DAY!**—arrive to **CRUSH** the Serpent's head?!

Time passed, and Sarah had no child. In fact, she had become far, far too old to have a baby. But the Mighty One had promised . . .

Then one day Sarah conceived (became pregnant) and she gave birth to a son, and they named him Isaac.

Question: Have you ever heard of a hundred-year-old woman giving birth? I know you have not. Sarah's baby is a miracle. Miracles are not difficult for the Mighty One, because He is Lord over all Creation. He made the world out of nothing. So it is not surprising that He makes Isaac from a man and woman who are way too old to have babies.

CHAPTER EIGHT

THE WOOD, THE FIRE, AND THE KNIFE

From THE BOOK CALLED GENESIS

GENESIS

BRAHAM AND SARAH LOVED ISAAC, their miracle baby from the Mighty One. On Isaac depended the great promise that Abraham's descendants would be like the stars in the sky—too many to count.

Question: What two things had the Mighty One promised Abraham? What?! You can't remember?! Okay, I know there's a lot to absorb, but you shouldn't blame me for quizzing you—no, you should not!

Answer: *Land* and *descendants*. Good heavens, a lot depends on Isaac! As Abraham and Sarah's only son, he **MUST** grow up to have children, or how will the Mighty One's promise of descendants ever be fulfilled?

Isaac grew.

And the Mighty One called to Abraham: "Abraham!" Abraham answered, "Here I am." The Mighty One said, "Take your only son, Isaac, and offer him up as a burnt offering on the mountain I will show you."

I can hear you shouting: "**WHAT**! This is horrible!" Yes, I know, but unless you keep reading you won't learn what it means.

The next morning Abraham saddled his donkey; he took with him two servants and his only son, Isaac, and the wood to build the fire for a burnt offering. Together they traveled to the mountain. On **THE THIRD DAY**—(remember these words "*the third day*" and add them to your list of *key words*, along with the number *three*)—Abraham looked up and saw the mountain the Mighty One had described. He said to his servants, "Stay here with the donkey, while I and the boy go up that mountain. We will worship the Mighty One and then return to you." (Did you *get* that? Abraham said that he and Isaac would *return*. How can Isaac return if his father is going to *sacrifice* him? Ah, the *Ancient Manual* is giving us hints about the outcome of this frightening story . . .)

Abraham bound the wood for the burnt offering to Isaac's back and Abraham carried the torch—and the knife. As they climbed, Isaac said to Abraham, "Father, we have the wood and the fire, but where is the lamb for the burnt offering?" Abraham answered, "My dear son, the Mighty One Himself will provide a lamb for the burnt offering."

When they reached the mountaintop, Abraham built an altar and arranged the wood on it. He bound Isaac, the one he loved, and laid him on top of the wood. Then he seized the knife to slaughter his son and immediately, while his arm was still raised, the Mighty One cried to him, "**ABRAHAM! ABRAHAM!**" Abraham wailed, "Here I am!" The Mighty One said, "Do not lay one hand on the boy! Do nothing to hurt him! Now I know that you revere the Mighty One—for you have not withheld from me your son, your only son, Isaac."

Abraham dropped the deadly knife and fell to the ground. When he raised his eyes, he saw a ram with its horns caught in a tangle of thick shrubs. So he offered the ram on the altar in place of Isaac. And he named that mountaintop "The Mighty One Will Provide."

The Mighty One called again to Abraham, saying, "Abraham, because you were willing to give me your most valuable possession, your only son, I will bless you beyond description. Your descendants will be like the stars in the night sky: too many to count. Through them, all the soil-creatures of Earth will be blessed because you heard my voice and obeyed me." (Oh, my! Did you see all the *key words* from the original Creation story?)

Let me explain. All the people in Ur, the city Abraham and Sarah had left, and all the wicked Canaanites who resided in the Land of Promise (Abraham and Sarah were now *surrounded* by Canaanites!), well, they all believed it was a good thing to sacrifice children to the so-called gods. This was one of the most horrendous lies the Sea Serpent had ever told them. Perhaps Abraham thought it was normal for the Mighty One to ask him to offer up Isaac—after all, that's what the so-called gods asked them to do. But it was not "normal" for the Mighty One at all! He is the God of Life, not death! He *never* wants death, and certainly not for parents to sacrifice their children!

Perhaps the Mighty One wanted to know how much Abraham trusted Him. Perhaps He also wanted to show Abraham that He, the Mighty One, does not (I repeat: **DOES NOT!**) want any children sacrificed **AT ALL, EVER!** Perhaps He was showing Abraham that the practice of sacrificing children **HAD TO STOP!** The evil so-called gods might require it, but the One True God **ABHORS** (hates) **IT**. Yes, I know—it's a thorny story to grasp; and it took place thousands of years ago in a far away land, among a people whose ways we cannot begin to understand. But what we do know is that Abraham showed the Mighty One that he, Abraham, trusted the God of Heaven and Earth, trusted Him **COMPLETELY**. He believed that if he did sacrifice Isaac, the Mighty One would raise Isaac back to life again—because the Mighty One *promised* that *through Isaac* would come too many descendants to count, and through all those descendants the Mighty One would bless the entire Earth.

SECRETS
of the
ANCIENT
MANUAL
REVEALED!

64

HEBREWS 11:17-19

MOTHER: SECRET AGENT

From THE BOOK CALLED EXODUS

EXODUS

ISAAC (WHO WAS *NOT* SACRIFICED ON THE MOUNTAIN) grew up and married his beautiful cousin Rebekah. Rebekah bore him twin sons: Esau and Jacob. It is Jacob's story we must follow, for it is *Jacob's* descendants who lead us to the *special descendant* of Eve.

Jacob had **TWELVE** sons (remember that number *twelve*; add it to your list of *key words*). Their names were (count them): Gad, Asher, Simeon, Reuben (like the sandwich), Issachar, Levi (like the blue jeans), Judah, Dan, Naphtali, Zebulun, Joseph, and Benjamin.

Jacob, father of the TWELVE, SPOKE with the Mighty One, even WRESTLED Him (I am not making this up)! After their wrestling match, the Mighty One named him Israel (it means "wrestled with God"). Whenever you encounter the name Israel, it refers to Jacob. Jacob, Israel, they're the *same man*—the SAME MAN—got that?

Jacob's (Israel's) TWELVE sons and their wives had scores of children and grandchildren. The entire clan herded its flocks in the Land of Promise (the land the Mighty One prepared for them, for they are Abraham's descendants). That is, until a devastating famine ravaged that part of the world for *seven* long years, spreading right across the face of the Earth. Jacob's (Israel's) enormous family had no bread. But there was bread in Egypt, stored in vast warehouses. There was no other choice to make: they left the Land of Promise for Egypt, taking everything they possessed. If it hadn't been for food in Egypt, Abraham's descendants would have PERISHED. The bread stored in Egypt was the Mighty One's provision, for He had promised that through Abraham's offspring He would bless the entire world. He could *not* let them die.

They settled in Egypt, with lush grazing land for their herds, and the Mighty One *blessed* them there. They were *fruitful* and *multiplied*. Each of Jacob's (Israel's) TWELVE sons had so many grandchildren, great-grandchildren, and great-great-grandchildren, the *Israelites* (for that is what I shall now call them) grew into TWELVE giant *tribes*: the TWELVE TRIBES OF ISRAEL. The famine had abated, the Israelites were well-fed, and except for being separated from their Land of Promise, life in Egypt was good.

Until a change in monarchy changed everything. A new pharaoh (king) came to power in Egypt. He knew nothing about the Israelites and their quiet history in Egypt. All he saw was that there were a lot of them, and I mean **A LOT**—too many to count!

Pharaoh said to his officials, "The Israelites are too strong for us. What if they rebel and join our enemies? We must weaken them." So Pharaoh put task masters over them, making the Israelites his labor slaves. But the more ruthlessly he treated them, the more they *multiplied*. Pharaoh quaked in fear, so he worked the Israelites even harder.

Then Pharaoh commanded: "Drown every male Israelite baby age two and under in the River Nile." Oh, the horror! Pharaoh reasoned that if he killed the Israelites' sons, there would be no Israelite warriors to attack Egypt.

EXODUS 1;
EXODUS 2:1-10

67

At that very time, an Israelite couple waited anxiously for the arrival of their second child: a boy. He was beautiful. His mother couldn't bear to throw him into the River Nile. Acting as the Mighty One's **SECRET AGENT**, she defied Pharaoh's law and hid her baby at home for *THREE* months. (Those *THREE* months of hiding remind us of Abraham and Isaac's *THREE-DAY* journey in the previous chapter—a journey toward death. During these *THREE* months of hiding, this brave mother's beautiful son is presumed **DEAD**—drowned in the Nile.) Well, suspicions mounted; danger surrounded the hiding place; so the mother made a tiny ark (an **ARK!**) woven from papyrus stalks, and she waterproofed it with tar. Putting her precious son into the ark (talk about a treasure chest!), she slipped the tiny craft ever so silently into the river, hidden among the reeds along the shore. And she stationed the baby's older sister a small distance away, to keep watch.

One of Pharaoh's daughters went down to the Nile to bathe and she spied the basket floating among the reeds. Inside was the baby, crying. "This must be one of the Israelite babies," she said, and her heart filled with pity for the helpless boy. Quickly, the baby's sister ran to the princess and said, "Shall I go and get an Israelite woman to nurse him for you?"

"Oh, yes!" said the princess. So the girl ran and got her own mother. The princess said, "Please nurse this baby for me. I will pay you for your work." And that is what the mother did; she nursed her own son until he was weaned. And when the time was right, she took him back to the princess, who adopted him. The princess named him Moses (it means "taken out of the water"). He grew up in Pharaoh's household, a prince of Egypt.

Reader, do you grasp what just happened? It gives me chills! You see, the baby Moses was **SAVED** from the waters of the Nile just as Noah and his people were **SAVED** from the waters of the great flood. Using two arks—and through the obedience of Noah, and Moses' secret-agent mother—the Mighty One saved these soil-creatures from watery graves; and by saving *them*, He will eventually save the whole world.

IMPORTANT INFORMATION: The River Nile represented Egypt's power to water its fields and grow crops. The Egyptians believed the Nile was inhabited by so-called gods that gave them everything they needed. There is, of course, only One True God, the Mighty One, who gives everyone breath and life and food. Just as the people of Noah's time had forgotten all about the Mighty One and bowed down to false gods, the people of Moses' time had also forgotten the Mighty One. They, too, bowed down to false gods. In this story, think of the River Nile just as you thought of the City of Ur—as a remnant of the old Sea of Chaos, full of wicked dragons that oppose the Mighty One.

While Moses was growing up—a prince of Egypt—his people, the Israelites, were worked to the bone by Pharaoh. In fact, by Moses' day, the Israelites had worked as labor slaves in Egypt for **HUNDREDS OF YEARS**. Centuries have passed since they first journeyed to Egypt to find bread.

Question: Could there be, oh, I dunno, **DRAGONS** behind Pharaoh's wicked schemes?

Answer: Oh, yes, there be **DRAGONS!** In particular: Rendagon, Morhgall, and Malefactor. (Learn about these monsters in my book *Dragon Slayers*.)

One day Prince Moses, who was now fully grown, went out to visit his people, and he witnessed an Egyptian slave master beating one of the Israelites. Unspeakable hate welled up inside Moses, who **MURDERED** the slave driver and buried the body in the sand. But someone saw the awful deed, and when Pharaoh heard of it, he ordered Moses' execution. Running for his life, Moses escaped to the land of Midian, where he worked quietly as a humble shepherd for many long years.

EXODUS 2:11-12

During those years the pharaoh of Egypt died, but the next pharaoh was just as much a tyrant; he worked the Israelites hard. They cried to the Mighty One: "Save us! Our masters whip us cruelly!" The Mighty One heard their groans and raised up a deliverer: Moses. **MOSES!**

One day while Moses tended his flocks in Midian, he came to Mount Horeb, which was later called the Mountain of God (remember this mountain!). There he saw a strange sight: tongues of fire leapt from a bush, yet the bush did not burn up. He crept closer. From the burning bush, the Mighty One called to him: "Moses! Moses!" He answered, "Here I am." The Mighty One said, "Come no closer, Moses, and remove your sandals, for you are standing on

EXODUS 3:1-15

holy ground." Trembling, he removed his sandals and waited. The Mighty One **SPOKE** again: "I am the God of your ancestors Abraham, Isaac, and Jacob." Moses buried his face in his arms, for he was terrified to look upon the One True God.

The Mighty One said to him, "I have heard the cries of my people enslaved in Egypt and have witnessed their **SUFFERING**. I have come down to deliver them from Pharaoh, to bring them out of that **DARK** and deadly place, back to the good **LAND** of Promise. Go now to Pharaoh and tell him to release the Israelites from their bondage."

Moses cried out: "Who am I to go to Pharaoh? Who am I to lead the Israelites out of Egypt?"

The Mighty One said, "I will go with you, Moses. When you lead the Israelites out of Egypt, you will bring them *here*, to this *very mountain* where I am speaking to you from this burning bush. Here my people will be free to worship me."

Moses said, "What if I go to the Israelites and they ask me your name? What shall I say?"

The Mighty One said, "**I AM WHO I AM.** Say to them '*I AM* sent me to deliver you.' I will send Aaron, your brother, to help you speak to Pharaoh."

IMPORTANT INFORMATION: The "Mighty One" is a general term, more of a title really, for the One True God. It is not a personal name, such as your own name. For example, I could call you "Dragon Slayer" or "reader," but these are mere titles; neither one of them is your *name*. Moses asked the Mighty One for His *personal name*—which was quite bold of Moses, don't you think? After all, who is Moses, a mere soil-creature, approaching the Mighty One with such an up-close and personal demand? Well, do you recall my telling you that the

Mighty One is *knowable* and wants very much to be known by *us?* He does. Which makes Moses' question quite reasonable. Do you not want to know the name of your own friend?

Here's what I think happened: When Moses asked the Mighty One for His *name*, the Mighty One understood that Moses *really truly wanted to know Him*. Not since the Garden of Delights has anyone known the Mighty One well enough to know His name. He gladly said to Moses, "My name is *I AM*."

I can hear what you're saying: "Well, what kind of a name is *that*?!" Ah, my friends, it is the greatest name of all! It means "*I AM* the One who exists, the One in whom all existence begins, the One through whom all existence continues." *That's* what kind of a name it is!

From here forward, I shall often use the Mighty One's personal name as I retell stories from the *Manual*. That does **NOT** mean, however, that I will cease saying "the Mighty One." No, no! It is a most important title. Sometimes I will say "the Mighty One" and sometimes I will call Him "*I AM*." It's a bit like "Jacob" and "Israel"—two names for the same person.

Are you wondering why I, Sir Wyvern Pugilist, should possess the arrogance—nay, the presumption—to call the Mighty One by His personal name? Why, it is not arrogant at all, because when He revealed His name to Moses, He revealed it to **ALL SOIL-CREATURES**, including *you* and *me*. To those who long to know Him, who is the Maker and Lover of their souls, He moves in close and whispers into their hearts, "*I AM* the one who loves you! *I AM* the great *I AM*."

CHAPTER TEN

BLOOD AND FREEDOM

From THE BOOK CALLED EXODUS

EXODUS

MOSES AND AARON SPOKE to the half-starved Israelites in Egypt: "The God of our ancestors, the God who appeared to Abraham, Isaac, and Jacob, has spoken also to us, and He has sent us to lead you out of this cruel bondage. The Mighty One's name is *I AM*. That is who has sent us to you." When the Israelites learned that the God of their ancestors had heard their cries for help *and* had revealed His name to them, they fell to their faces and worshiped Him.

Then Moses and Aaron went to Pharaoh and said: "This is what *I AM*, the God of our ancestors, says to you: 'LET MY PEOPLE GO!'"

EXODUS 5:1-23

Pharaoh sneered. "Who is this *I AM* that I should listen to him? No, I will not let the Israelites go!" Pharaoh told his slave drivers, "These slaves are lazy and whining. Instead of providing them straw for making bricks, let them gather their own straw. Command them to produce the same number of bricks. Then they'll learn what real work is!"

When the Israelites couldn't make the same number of bricks in the same time as before, their masters whipped them. The despondent slaves cried to Pharaoh, "How can we make bricks with no straw? It is your fault we fall behind—because we have no straw."

73

Pharaoh growled, "You lazy servants! Get back to work! Gather your own straw!"

They returned to work, but first they railed against Moses and Aaron: "Look what you have done to us! To Pharaoh, we smell like rotten garbage! He wants to kill us! May the great *I AM* judge you for bringing such harm upon us!"

So Moses cried to *I AM*, saying, "O great *I AM*, why have you brought such hard trouble upon your people?!" And *I AM* said to Moses, "Watch what will happen; for because my hand is mighty, Pharaoh will let my people go."

EXODUS 7-11

The great *I AM* had given Moses a staff to carry, a staff through which *I AM* performed miracles in front of Pharaoh. When he met Pharaoh by the banks of the River Nile (yes, the very river from which Moses' life had been saved), Moses threw his staff on the ground and it turned into a snake. (A snake! Ooooh! Pharaoh believed in a snake-god and feared it!) It twisted on the ground, but when Moses picked it up, it became a staff again. Moses said to Pharaoh, "Because *I AM* said to you, 'Let my people go,' and you would not listen, see now what the great *I AM* will do." Then Moses struck the waters of the Nile with his staff, and the waters turned to blood. Everywhere in Egypt, rivers and pools turned to blood.

But Pharaoh refused to let the Israelites go.

Seven days later (*seven days*: *key words, key words!*) Moses returned to Pharaoh and said, "The great *I AM* says, **'LET MY PEOPLE GO!'**" But once again the hard-hearted Pharaoh refused. Then Aaron took Moses' staff and stretched it out over all the streams and ponds in Egypt; ugly frogs came up from the muddy waters and covered the land. Hop, hop, hop—they hopped everywhere, even into people's ovens.

After that, Aaron took the staff and struck the dust of the ground, and all over Egypt the dust became swarming gnats.

But Pharaoh refused to let the Israelites go.

The great *I AM* sent hordes of flies into Egypt; they swarmed the palace; they devastated the fields.

But Pharaoh refused to let the Israelites go.

The great *I AM* sent a plague on Egypt's livestock, all the cattle, sheep, and goats, all the donkeys, horses, and camels.

But Pharaoh refused to let the Israelites go.

Moses tossed a handful of soot from a furnace into the air, and suddenly the Egyptians were covered with painful, weeping skin sores.

But despite the people's cries, Pharaoh's heart hardened like stone and he refused to let the Israelites go.

Moses stretched his hand toward the sky, and the great *I AM* sent a howling storm—thunder and lightning, and hail that pummeled the fields—more terrifying than anyone had ever seen.

But Pharaoh refused to let the Israelites go.

Moses stretched out his hand over Egypt, and the great *I AM* sent locusts: the sky was black with them; the ground was black with them; they gobbled up every green plant that had not been destroyed by the hail. They stripped the mighty land of Egypt bare.

But Pharaoh refused to let the Israelites go.

Moses stretched his hand toward the sky and a plague of DARKNESS covered the LAND for THREE whole DAYS. The darkness was so intense that a person could feel it, for the DARKNESS was as DARK as the grave.

But Pharaoh refused to let the Israelites go.

STOP! I must tell you something about these horrific plagues. Each of them has something to do with the so-called gods that Pharaoh worshiped. Do not think of the plagues as nasty punishments the Mighty One imposed to "get even" with Pharaoh. No, no, no. In the plagues, the One True God, Creator and Sustainer of all Life, opposes and defeats Egypt's false gods. The frog-goddess, the river-god, the snake-god, the earth-god, the storm-god, the harvest-goddess, the darkness-god, the healing-goddess, the death-god—in the face of the great *I AM*, they are exposed for what they are: false and powerless.

Moses said to Pharaoh, "*I AM* says to you: 'At midnight I will pass through Egypt, and every firstborn male in Egypt will die; rich and poor alike; people and animals alike. There will be weeping and wailing greater than you have ever heard.'"

But Pharaoh was not moved.

Moses and Aaron said to the Israelites, "Here is what *I AM* says: 'Take lambs, one for each family. Slaughter the lambs at twilight and take the blood and paint it on the door frames of your houses. Roast the lambs; then go inside your houses to eat the meat. Eat it with unleavened bread, because there is no time for leavening. Be dressed for travel when you eat: wear your cloaks and your sandals; have your bags packed. During the night, I will pass through Egypt, and when I see the blood of the lambs painted on your door posts I will *pass over* you. The death angel shall not visit your houses.'"

At midnight the great *I AM* passed through Egypt, and the firstborn male in every household died. But where the blood of the lambs was painted on the door posts, the death angel *passed over* that house. Among Pharaoh's people, there was weeping and wailing louder than anyone had ever heard. "Go!" Pharaoh raged at Moses. "Take your people and your animals! Leave Egypt!" So the Israelites fled Egypt, and no one tried to stop them. They marched out according to their TWELVE tribes—thousands upon thousands of Israelites, because they had been FRUITFUL and MULTIPLIED.

That night, *I AM* delivered His people from bondage. He commanded them: "Every year, from this time forward, you shall celebrate the Feast of Passover. Here is how you shall celebrate it: For seven days (*seven days*!) you must eat unleavened bread, but the *seventh day* itself will be a festival to the great *I AM*. Tell your children, 'We do this so we will never forget that *I AM* freed us from our bondage in Egypt.'"

Dragon Slayers, I want you to know something. We are soooo much like the ancient Israelites, for each of us also lives in bondage, bondage to the lies of the Sea Serpent and Deathbreath's cruel claws. The whole world lies under the tyranny of their vile schemes. When the Mighty One led the Israelites out of Egypt (the event is called the *Exodus*), He took another giant step in His Grand Plan to rescue the world from dragons. For it is through those enslaved *Israelites* that the Mighty One will send the special descendant of Eve, who will one day—**ONE DAY!**—destroy the Serpent and Deathbreath. When the Israelites escaped a "sea of evil" in Egypt, they *foreshadowed* the future escape of the whole world from the Sea of Chaos and its devastating monsters.

BLOOD
AND
FREEDOM

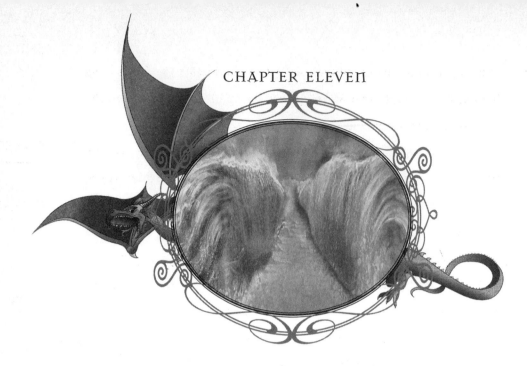

CHAPTER ELEVEN

THE SEA RETREATS

From THE BOOKS CALLED EXODUS *and* LEVITICUS

EXODUS
AND
LEVITICUS

JACOB'S (ISRAEL'S) DESCENDANTS WALKED FREE. Hundreds of thousands of them, maybe over a million. Together with their flocks and herds, they marched out of Egypt and not one person tried to stop them. Many Egyptians, as well as some other foreign settlers, had come to believe in *I AM,* and they left with them, for they, too, longed to be freed from bondage, bondage to Egypt's false gods. It seemed as if a large part of the world was freed that night, soil-creatures from all walks of life, rich and poor alike, from many nations.

EXODUS 13:20-22   The Mighty One, whose secret name is *I AM,* guided them on a desert road to the Red Sea. His Presence was visible in a pillar of cloud by day and a pillar of fire by night. He never left their sight, and His fire (like the flames in the burning bush) dispelled the **DARKNESS**. Even the **DARK** is not **DARK** to the Mighty One, for He shines as bright as the day. ("Let there be **LIGHT!**")

Meanwhile, Pharaoh again changed his mind. He said to his advisors, "What have we done letting the Israelites go?! We've lost our labor slaves! Hunt them down!"

Pharaoh readied 600 of his best chariots, their horses and their drivers. "Pursue the Israelites!" he commanded. "Haul them back to Egypt!"

Thundering Egyptian armies raced toward the Red Sea, but the Israelites cried to their *I AM*: "Save us! Here come the Egyptians!"

Moses said to them: "Fear not! Stand firm, all of you. You will never see these Egyptian warriors again. Today the great *I AM* will fight for you."

Moses held out his arm toward the Red Sea, and the frightful Sea divided, for the Mighty One blew His **BREATH** across it like a strong **EAST** wind, driving the waters back, until dry **LAND** appeared. (Reader, do you see what's happening? It's just like *in the beginning*, when the Mighty One blew His **BREATH** across the Sea of Chaos, driving it back! His plan to re-create the **EARTH** is moving forward. He wants to deliver *all* **SOIL-CREATURES** from the **DARK SEA**, and He begins by delivering His own people from the Red **SEA**—and from slavery and death in Egypt.) The Israelites passed through the **SEA**, with a wall of water on their right and a wall of water on their left, but the **GROUND** they stepped on was dry. All night long, Moses held his arm stretched out to the **SEA**, and all night long the Mighty One commanded the deadly **SEA** to retreat.

The Egyptian armies followed the Israelites into the **SEA** bed, with the walls of water standing on their right and on their left. After the Israelites crossed safely to the other side, Moses lowered his arm, and the **SEA** returned, covering the vicious armies. Not one Egyptian warrior survived. It was a day of both joy and grief—joy over the Israelites' escape from bondage, grief over the Egyptian warriors' demise, grief over Pharaoh's rock-hard heart that drove them to their watery graves.

Then the Israelites regarded the Mighty One, their *I AM*, with reverence and awe. They trusted Him, and they trusted His servant Moses.

But soon they grumbled. They looked around and saw only desert. They complained to Moses: "Why have you brought us out here to die? At least we had food in Egypt."

Give me a **BREAK!** Can you *believe* these whiners? Why, it's only been a **FEW DAYS** since they were (**MIRACULOUSLY**) delivered from the most horrendous bondage. All that they had ever known in Egypt was slavery, and now they want to go back for the **FOOD?** Oh, **PULEEZE!** If I were the Mighty One (and it's a good thing I'm not), I would have abandoned them right then and there!

EXODUS 34:6

O the Mighty One, merciful and compassionate, slow to anger, and abounding in lovingkindness! (That's a direct quote from the *Ancient*

EXODUS 16:1-15

Manual.) He heard their cries and sent them food. Every morning, bread from heaven appeared all over the ground. They marveled and said, "What is it?" So they named it manna, which means "what is it?" Imagine this scene every morning in the desert: the Israelites yawn, rub their eyes, then look outside their tents. All over the ground is this strange-looking bread. They say to each other, "Oh, yum! There's more of that delicious 'what is it?'" Each family passes it around their breakfast gathering and Mother says, "Here—have some more 'what is it?' Remember that 'what is it?' does not last all day. You must eat it now, before it gets moldy."

Then every evening, the Mighty One sent flocks of birds called quail, so the Israelites had meat for dinner; and when they found no water to drink, the Mighty One ordered water to gush from rocks. All the while they were in the desert, they never lacked bread or meat or water, because the Mighty One satisfied their every need. Well, of course He did! He is the great *I AM*, the *source* of all that *exists*!

Three months (it reminds me of the *three months* Moses was hidden by his secret-agent mother!) after the Mighty One rescued the Israelites from Egypt they came to Mount Horeb, the Mountain of God, the *very place* where the Mighty One had spoken to Moses from the burning bush, the *very place* where He had said to him, "My name is *I AM*." Moses remembered what *I AM* had told him there: "When you lead the Israelites out of Egypt, you will bring them to this very mountain."

At the base of Mount Horeb, the TWELVE TRIBES OF ISRAEL (these freed slaves, all the descendants of Abraham, Isaac, and Jacob/Israel) set up camp.

Moses ascended Mount Horeb alone. There the Mighty One said to him, "Go down and say to the Israelites: 'If you obey my Words and follow me completely, then you will be my treasure. The whole Earth is mine, but you will be special—you will be a nation of priests, worshiping the One True God, set aside for my purposes.'"

When Moses SPOKE the Mighty One's Words to the Israelites, they shouted as with one voice: "We will obey all the Words of the Mighty One!"

The Mighty One said to Moses, "Tell the people to cleanse themselves, and to not draw too close to the mountain, because in THREE DAYS [*three days!*] I will come down to Earth, to the top of Mount Horeb. Tell them to stay far back, for the mountain is too holy for them to touch."

On the *third day* it happened. The ground shook, thunder rumbled from afar, escalating into resounding booms, coming closer, right to the mountain itself, which trembled violently. The mountain quaked, unfastening jagged boulders that tumbled to the valley below, while a dense cloud descended, like a shroud of terrifying night, and javelins of lightning rent the skies. Smoke belched from the mountaintop, as if from a massive furnace, and flames licked the sky. A trumpet blared, but no one saw a trumpet player.

The Mighty One **SPOKE** to them from the fire, just as He **SPOKE** to Moses from the burning bush, just as He **SPOKE** the Creation into existence.

Never forget that when the Mighty One *SPEAKS*, **LIFE** and **GOODNESS** happen! The Mighty One's **WORD** is powerful; it is *active*; it causes things to *be*; it declares *truth*. This time when He **SPOKE**, the Mighty One revealed His own character, summing it up in **TEN LAWS, TEN WORDS** from the Mighty One's heart. These Ten Laws not only reveal who *He* is, they also reveal who *we* are *supposed* to be. Do you recall that **SOIL-CREATURES** were made *IN THE IMAGE* of the Mighty One? Of course you do. In our original state, we were made to be *like* the Mighty One, to *represent His character on* **EARTH**. After the awful **SERPENT** entered the **GARDEN OF DELIGHTS**, we forgot so much about the Mighty One—and ourselves. Now the Israelites will be *told* by the Mighty One Himself what *He* is like—and what *we* should be like, too. The Ten **GOOD** Laws—the Ten Good **WORDS**—**SPOKEN** to Moses will teach the Israelites, and *us*, how to forsake **EVIL** and **LIVE** in love with the Mighty One and each other. The Ten Laws tell us what **LIFE** looked like *before* the **SERPENT** entered our world, and what **LIFE** will look like *again* when the **SERPENT** and Deathbreath are one day—**ONE DAY!**—

defeated by the special DESCENDANT of Eve. (Yes, I helped you underline the *key words* above. I DO hope you're keeping up with your ASSIGNMENT.)

Here, then, are the Ten Good Laws, SPOKEN by the Mighty One Himself. (You really should MEMORIZE them! C'mon, EVERYONE knows them! Even if you say you don't, you do, because you already know them *by instinct*, in your *heart*, because the Mighty One made you *in His image*.)

1. *I AM your God, who led you out of a land of bondage. You shall have no other "gods" before me.*
2. *Make no idols from wood or stone; make no image of anything in heaven or Earth to bow down to in worship.*
3. *Do not misuse my personal name: I AM.*
4. *On the seventh day of every week, rest. Work for six days, but rest on the seventh, because in six days I created the world, and on the seventh day I rested. I blessed the seventh day and made it holy.*
5. *Honor your mother and your father, so that it will go well for you in your new land.*
6. *No murder.*
7. *No adultery.*
8. *No stealing.*
9. *No lying about your neighbor.*
10. *No coveting anything that belongs to your neighbor.*

EXODUS 20:1-17

83

The people trembled at the sight of the smoke, the lightning, the fire, and the sound of the Mighty One's voice, and they drew back. But Moses went up the mountain once again because the Mighty One called him there, and Moses drew near to the thick darkness, for the Mighty One was in that darkness.

EXODUS 20:21

Moses remained on the mountaintop for many, many days while the Mighty One taught him how to govern the people and how to lead them back to the **LAND** He had promised their ancestor Abraham. In addition to the Ten Laws, the Mighty One gave Moses *more* Laws to teach to the people: *Love your neighbor as you love yourself*; and *Never neglect the widows, the orphans, or the alien foreigners among you. For you were once aliens in Egypt.*

Let me explain something. In the ancient world, widows, orphans, and foreign aliens were the poorest of the poor. There was no one—I repeat: **NO ONE**—to give them food, shelter, and clothing. That is why the Mighty One specifically commanded His people to care for these outcasts, because He **LOVES** the outcasts and the poor. Are you an outcast? Are you poor? Do you not have a parent? This special Law is for you, it's for you! The Mighty One calls to *you*, speaking to *you*, using His personal name, saying "*I AM* the One who loves you. *I AM* your parent. *I AM* the One who will never leave you."

The multitude of freed slaves was now a nation—the Mighty One's nation. They had *sworn* to *obey* the Mighty One's **WORDS**; they would be a kingdom of priests, worshiping the One True God, Creator of all things; and they would **BLESS** all the nations of **EARTH** by pointing them to the great *I AM*, who made them and loves them and longs to be known by them.

With His own finger, the Mighty One inscribed the Ten Laws on two stone tablets for Moses to give to the people.

But weeks passed, and Moses remained on the mountain, talking one-on-one with *I AM*, his very best friend. (Well, of course he remained up there! If the Mighty One invited *you* up the mountain for a personal talk, would you *ever* want to leave? No way! Moses was on that mountaintop *WALKING AND TALKING* with the Mighty One Himself, even calling Him by *name*!) The people

LEVITICUS 19:18

EXODUS 22:21-22;
EXODUS 23:9

84

grew restless. They said to Aaron, "Moses has disappeared! Who knows if he'll ever come back! Now then, make us a god to worship."

Appallingly, Aaron collected the Israelites' gold jewelry, melted it down, EXODUS 32:1-4 and from it fashioned a statue of a calf (like the calf-god in Egypt!). The people bowed before the golden calf and worshiped it, claiming it was—oh, it is so deplorable. I can almost not speak it—claiming it was the great *I AM*. (I shudder.)

At last, Moses descended the mountain, carrying the two stone tablets in his arms. He saw the people singing and dancing before the golden calf, bowing down in worship to it. "What is this sound of unholy singing?!" he raged, and his anger burned against the people just as it had burned against Pharaoh and his so-called gods. In wrath, he threw the stone tablets to the ground and they shattered into pieces.

I'm relieved to report that the people repented of their awful deed and the Mighty One made another set of stone tablets on which He inscribed the Ten Laws. But this incident of the golden calf . . . it was the most **HORRIBLE** thing they could have done, and they did not act alone. I must tell you (because I have promised to tell you the truth about the world) that the devious and loathsome **SERPENT** was behind it, as well as its dreaded companion.

Dear reader, do you see what's happened? The Israelites *swore* to obey all of the Mighty One's *Words*. What were His *first Words* to them, in the Ten Good Laws? *I AM your God, who led you out of a land of bondage. You shall have no other "gods" before me.* So what do the Israelites do? They **BREAK** their promise by **DISREGARDING** the *very first words* the Mighty One **SPOKE** to them! They invent a so-called golden-calf god and **WORSHIP IT!** Do their actions not remind you of Adam and Eve, when they first listened to the stinking **SEA SERPENT**? Yes. The Israelites *reject* the Mighty One's powerful

WORDS, thus turning their backs on **LIFE** and **TRUTH!** Oh, I hate to tell you

what happened next, but I must. Deathbreath invaded the Israelites' camp

and struck down many of those promise-breaking, God-rejecting people. For

where the God of Life is absolutely refused, the doors are thrown wide open to

the Serpent's closest companion, and all that's left is . . . well, death.

SECRETS
of the
ANCIENT
MANUAL
REVEALED!

THE PRESENCE IN THE WILDERNESS

From THE BOOK CALLED EXODUS

EXODUS

P RIVATELY, MOSES CRIED OUT to the Mighty One, calling Him by His secret name. "O great *I AM*," he pleaded, "how can I lead these people? They are ornery and rebellious. They are slow to seek you and obey you. I cannot do this work alone. Who will you send with me to help me lead them back to the Land of Promise?"

I AM answered Moses, saying, "Do not fear, Moses. My own Presence will go with you, and I will give you rest."

So Moses led the people away from Mount Horeb and they continued their trek to the Land of Promise. And the Mighty One's own Presence remained with them and guided them throughout their long journey. When His Presence moved ahead of them, leading them in the pillar of cloud and fire, they moved forward. When His Presence stopped, they stopped and set up their camp.

STOP! Are you wondering what I'm wondering? You *are?* Ha! I *knew* it! We're all thinking, **WELL**, if there's a campground, there must be *tents*, and if there are tents, we can only assume that every family has its own. So then, *where* is the Mighty One living? He's come to be with Moses and the Israelites as they travel, and you mean to tell me that *He*, of all beings, **HAS NO TENT?!** Oh dear, oh dear! This is **NOT** what any self-respecting Israelite would call hospitality. Are they not going to provide a **TENT** for the Mighty One?

Yes.

EXODUS 26-27

The Mighty One *will* have His own tent, and soon. Once again He **SPOKE** to Moses, giving him detailed instructions for crafting a very special, very sacred lodging for the Mighty One's own dwelling. Of course, no tent can contain the Mighty One, the God of the whole Universe! And yet, the God of the whole Universe was pleased to make His Presence especially known in this extraordinary shelter. According to the Mighty One's precise directions, the people worked together to construct it. From their **TWELVE TRIBES**, they summoned weavers, and artists who worked in gold and silver and bronze—all the precious metals the Egyptians gave them on the night the Mighty One delivered them from bondage. They wove fine linen cloths for curtains; they tanned hides of goat hair for coverings; they created fabrics containing golden threads and dyes of bright blue, purple, and red; they fashioned tables and altars, a lamp stand, and bowls and platters overlaid with gold and silver.

Guess what else they made? Ach! You'll **NEVER** guess, never in a million years, so I shall tell you. They built an **ARK!** (This is now the **THIRD ARK** we've encountered in the *Ancient Manual*.) It was not nearly as large as Noah's ark, and it was not nearly as tiny as Moses' ark. My guess is that it was a bit larger than the one in which Moses' secret-agent mother hid him in the River Nile. This new and very particular ark—because it was the **MOST HOLY ARK** of all arks that ever were or ever shall be—was overlaid with **GOLD!** As are all arks, it was a *treasure chest*. Can you guess what *exalted treasure* was placed inside it? Of course you can't! Because I have not told you, and I'm not going to—not yet. I cannot reveal all the *Manual's* secrets at once, can I? **HEAVENS NO!** You must keep reading. (Hint: This particular ark did not contain soil-creatures.)

When at last the artisans finished creating all the beautiful pieces, they assembled them and pitched the sacred tent . . . Well, I'm not going to tell you where they pitched it—not quite yet.

IMPORTANT INFORMATION: When the Israelites began their journey to the Land of Promise, Moses frequently met one-on-one with the Mighty One, boldly calling Him by His personal name *I AM*. Are you wondering *where* the two met each other? **THEY MET IN A TENT, OF COURSE!** Where else, in the middle of the desert, could you meet with someone *privately* if not in a tent? It was called the Tent of Meeting, and I think that was the perfect name for it, don't you? The Mighty One and Moses visited this tent at the same time, and that is where they talked together. Now, it's very important to know that the Tent of Meeting was pitched *outside* the Israelites' campground, because the

EXODUS 33:7-11

Mighty One was too holy for the Israelites to approach. So Moses approached the Mighty One alone—going outside the campground. Did you get that? The Tent of Meeting stood *outside the campground*. Now watch what happens.

As I was saying, the people assembled all the pieces and pitched the sacred *new* tent (the one in which the Mighty One would dwell) IN THE VERY CENTER OF THEIR CAMPGROUND. (Gasp!) The Mighty One is coming *so close* to them! They called God's new tent the Tabernacle (which means "tent" or "hut"). Then the Presence of the Mighty One *entered* the Tabernacle, and His astonishing glory FILLED IT and shone above it, in a pillar of cloud and fire. Grouped according to their TWELVE TRIBES, the Israelites then pitched their own tents in orderly rows surrounding the Tabernacle on its four sides.

Dragon Slayer, do you realize what's happened? The Mighty One first SPOKE to the Israelites from Mount Horeb, and they stood far away. Only Moses went up the mountain to meet the Mighty One. Then the Mighty One came closer to the people, visiting with Moses in the Tent of Meeting *outside* the campground. Now the Mighty One has moved to the *very center* of the camp. His own Presence filled the Tabernacle and now He would dwell *among* the people. Not since the invasion of the wicked SERPENT had the Mighty One lived so closely with SOIL-CREATURES. In fact, His Presence was now *so close*, there were times when the Israelites' campground seemed to be a tiny slice of the old GARDEN OF DELIGHTS.

Not only did the Mighty One abide in their midst in His own tent, He also told the Israelites, through Moses, how to use the Tabernacle as a portable temple—for that is what a temple is, a place where God comes to Earth to live among His soil-creatures. Can you imagine? A PORTABLE TEMPLE! Every time the TWELVE TRIBES broke camp, traveling toward the Land of Promise, the **PORTABLE TEMPLE** also moved—in fact, it *led* them. Whenever the pillar of cloud stood extra-high above the Tabernacle, the people knew the Mighty One was telling them to *move*. And move they did.

Oh, I can hear what you're asking. You're asking, "What on Earth goes on inside a *temple*?" A lot! Let me explain that the Tabernacle/Temple was not a *simple* tent, the type you sleep in when you go camping. No, no! It was *complex* and full of symbolism. Remember, no soil-creature thought it up—it was the Mighty One's idea and plan. Everything in the Tabernacle/Temple was laid out according to the Mighty One's careful directions.

Enclosed by an outer fence made of beautiful fabric hangings, there was a spacious courtyard lying before the Tabernacle/Temple itself. Here the priests and the people offered thank-you offerings and sin offerings on an **ALTAR**. **NOTE:** When you're in the courtyard you are not (I repeat: You are **NOT**) inside the Mighty One's tent! Well, how could you be? You're in a *yard* and a *yard* is outside! Where, then, is the tent itself? Where is the Tabernacle/Temple in which the Mighty One's Presence resides? Ah, my friend, that's where it gets more *complex*.

Pretend you're in the Tabernacle's large rectangular courtyard. Now walk toward the back of the courtyard. Do you see it—the tent? Yes, it looks like an ordinary rectangular tent, but there is nothing **ORDINARY** about it! It has two chambers. The first chamber—where you'll find yourself if you enter the tent—is called the Holy Place.

STOP! You're about to enter the tent, aren't you?! No, no, no! You **MUST NOT ENTER IT!** It is too holy, too "set apart" from common soil-creature life, because the Mighty One's Presence is inside there! Step away from the entrance! **NOW!**

Oh, I'm sorry, I didn't mean to frighten you—no, actually I did. You see, even the Mighty One's *own people* could not enter the Holy Place. Only the specially ordained *priests* could enter it, and only after they had truly cleansed themselves. The ritual baths they took were symbolic acts, showing that soil-creatures, because of the presence of evil in their lives, need to be cleansed of evil before they can hope to approach the Mighty One, in whom **NO** evil dwells.

Well then, let's pretend that you and I are ancient Israelite *priests* and we have just completed our ritual baths. Now we are clean enough to enter the Mighty One's Presence. So we *do* enter the Holy Place. In this chamber, we burn incense and offer prayers to the Mighty One on behalf of all the people. We also light the lamp stand—all **TWELVE** of its lamps—replenishing the olive oil to keep them burning day and night, because they represent the **TWELVE TRIBES** among whom the Mighty One now dwells. Through the **TWELVE** lights burning on the lamp stand, all **TWELVE TRIBES** *symbolically* come into the Holy Place (even though the priests are the only ones to *physically* enter it). Okay, stay with me now, because I'm about to tell you about the *second chamber* inside the tent, at the *back* of the Holy Place: It is the Most Holy Place. **STOP! DO NOT ENTER IT, DO NOT ENTER IT!** Yes, yes, I know you're a priest (pretending to be, and this is all in our imaginations), but did I ever say that *every* priest can enter the Most Holy Place? Did I? **NO I DID NOT!** You see, when you're dealing with the Tabernacle, the Mighty One's personal tent, His portable temple, you must be *very careful.* You are treading on **HOLY GROUND. PULEEZE DO NOT MOVE TOO QUICKLY! WAIT FOR INSTRUCTIONS!**

Out of all the priests in ancient Israel (there were many), there was only **ONE** high priest. Only the *high priest* can enter the Most Holy Place, and *only*

ONCE A YEAR. That's how holy the Most Holy Place is. Once a year, the *high priest*, after cleansing himself very carefully, and only in fear and trembling (because he is a mere soil-creature who has surely committed sin in his life, and he is about to enter the Presence of the sinless and holy God of the whole universe), enters the Most Holy chamber of the Tabernacle, carrying the life-blood from a slain lamb. In doing so, the *high priest* obtains forgiveness of sins from the Mighty One for the entire nation—the *entire nation*. Now you understand why I shouted at you: **DON'T GO IN THERE!**

I've kept a special surprise for you. I told you about a special box the artisans made when they were constructing the fabrics and furniture of the Tabernacle. It was an **ARK**—a *treasure chest*—covered with **GOLD**. I won't tell you—not yet—what treasure was placed inside that sacred **ARK**, but I will tell you where the **ARK** itself was placed. They kept it in . . . the **MOST HOLY PLACE**. That's where it sat. They called the **ARK** the Mighty One's throne, for it was above the **ARK** that the Presence of the Mighty One, visible as a pillar of cloud and fire, settled.

You cannot look upon the golden **ARK**—not yet. It sits in the Most Holy Place, and you are not the *high priest*. So then, because you are not, I want you to slowly and carefully *back away* from the entrance to that most holy chamber, and slowly and carefully *back out* of the chamber you're in—the Holy Place—until you are safely outside again, in the Tabernacle's open courtyard. Now you may leave the courtyard through its curtained door, and stroll back to your own tent. Phew! I am glad our tour has ended because I nearly fell over in a dead faint when I saw you attempting to enter the Most Holy Place. Let me rest for a minute, until my heart stops **RACING!**

ENTERING THE LAND OF PROMISE (MAYBE)

It did not take long for the Israelites to reach the borders of their Land of Promise, the LAND the Mighty One gave to Abraham's descendants. Oh, how long ago it was that Jacob (Israel) and his TWELVE SONS had left that very LAND to find bread in Egypt during the devastating famine. Over ten generations had since come and gone, and the LAND of Promise seemed now like an old myth. Not a single Israelite in Moses' multitude had ever seen the place! After 430 years of bondage in Egypt, Abraham's DESCENDANTS had at last come home.

Why, then, did they REFUSE to go in? Ah, they feared the land's evil inhabitants, the Canaanites, who worshiped false gods like those in Egypt, and who sacrificed their own children (the horror!) to those idols. Plus, Canaanite warriors were deadly vicious. After everything the Mighty One had done for the Israelites, freeing them from Egypt, feeding them with manna and quail, giving them water to drink, speaking to them from the top of Mount Horeb, even traveling with them in a tent, guiding, comforting, protecting, delivering them from every foe, loving them every second of every hour of every day, they *did not trust Him* to protect them from the ferocious Canaanites. CAN YOU BELIEVE IT?!

They had little faith, this generation of freed slaves. Ah, well. I should not be so hard on them. Many are the times when I, too, have little faith. (But for PETE'S SAKE!—Could they not trust the Mighty One *at all?)*

Back toward Egypt they turned—although they didn't go quite that far. 'Round and 'round the wilderness they wandered, like Cain living in the Land of Nod, for *FORTY* long years. (FORTY YEARS! Dragon Slayer, does that not remind you of Noah and his family in the ark for *forty days* and *forty nights*, waiting for the Mighty One to deliver them from the waters of death and to begin the Creation afresh?) The wandering Israelites grumbled and whined; they complained bitterly against the Mighty One, saying, "Why did you bring us out here to *die*?" (Oh, **PULEEZE!**) And, "In Egypt we had *meat* and *garlic*!" What?! Are you kidding me?! In Egypt they made bricks without straw, and were beaten, and probably ate gruel. Yet despite their **WHINING**, over and over, day in and day out, the Mighty One fed them with "what is it?" and quail and sweet water. For *forty years* their clothes did not rot and their sandals never knew holes. Did you get that?! Their clothes and sandals did **NOT WEAR OUT** for *forty years!* Try it—see if you can wear the same outfit and the same shoes for forty years. Ready . . . get set . . . go! (**NOTE:** I did not tell you to cease *washing* your clothes—just don't buy new ones.)

Reader, do you have any idea what happens across a span of *forty years?* You do **NOT**, because you haven't lived that long, so I shall tell you: Children are born and grow up, and old people die—curse the stinking Deathbreath! So at the end of *forty years* of wandering in the wilderness (wearing the same clothes and sandals), the freed slaves had seen most of their people (the ones who walked out of Egypt the night of the Exodus) *die*, and they saw a new generation of Israelites grow up, children who had *never even seen* Egypt, who knew *only* the harsh conditions of the desert—but who also knew the continual Presence of the Mighty One in their midst. These new **DESCENDANTS** of Abraham, Isaac, and Jacob/Israel were not whiners. Far from it! Since infancy, they had witnessed the Mighty One's miraculous provisions. Every morning of their lives they awakened to the pillar of cloud above the Tabernacle, and every night before they tucked themselves under their blankets they saw the pillar of fire: the Presence who was with them. Faith in the Mighty One FILLED THE HEARTS of these young men and women, Israel's greatest generation. It is this generation that reentered the Land of Promise. They were true Dragon Slayers.

CHAPTER THIRTEEN

A NEW GARDEN
OF DELIGHTS (NOT!)

From THE BOOKS CALLED DEUTERONOMY *and* JOSHUA

DEUTERONOMY
AND JOSHUA

I HOPE YOU HAVE NOT FORGOTTEN YOUR **ASSIGNMENT** to watch for *key words* from the earlier stories. I've been underlining some of them for you (which I really shouldn't do because I know you're quite capable), but I haven't underlined *all* of them. I fear you've been attacked by the dragon Slackbottom and are slacking off. **GET MOVING!**

FORTY *years* have passed since Abraham's **DESCENDANTS** escaped from Egypt, and now the new generation of dragon-slaying Israelites is camped outside the **LAND** of Promise, on the **EAST**ern bank of the Jordan River, awaiting the Mighty

One's commands. Look at your map, look at your map! They are camped *just outside* the Land of Promise! And I can hear all of you pestering me, shouting, "SIR WYVERN, WILL THEY ENTER THE LAND THIS TIME, WILL THEY? IF THEY DO, WILL THE WICKED CANAANITES KILL THEM? WE DON'T WANT THEM TO GET KILLED, BUT WE DON'T WANT THEM TO TURN BACK TO THAT AWFUL DESERT EITHER!"

Ach! You're killing my ears with your SHOUTING! I'm not telling you what happens—not yet. First I must tell you about Moses, who has led the people for *forty years* as they've wandered 'round and 'round the wilderness, whining and complaining. He's old and worn out and sick to death of all the grumbling!

The grumblers (the ones who are left) are also old. As I just told you, most of them have already died in the desert, and to *think* they could have been living all those years in the Land of Promise, if only they had trusted the Mighty One! I know full well they died of old age, but I also suspect that many of them died from . . . well, grrrumbling!

So, as the nation was camped on the *east* side of the Jordan River . . .

Let me interrupt myself to say something *key*: You'll recall that when Adam and Eve left the Garden of Delights they went *east*; their descendants are still *east* of the old Garden. But by going *west*, back to their good LAND of Promise, they're *hoping* to get back to the Garden. And aren't we all? Isn't that what all soil-creatures want? Is it not our hearts' desire to return to the Garden of Delights, to that time before the Serpent invaded?

Allow me to begin again . . . As the nation was camped on the *east* side of the Jordan River waiting for instructions from Moses, the Mighty One called Moses to come up, alone, to a mountaintop. From that great height, He showed Moses the Land of Promise's vast and beautiful expanse. I believe

Moses and *I AM* had a long and lovely conversation up there. After all, they liked to talk together on mountaintops. Was it not at the top of Mount Horeb that Moses and *I AM* talked together for *weeks*, when *I AM* gave Moses the Ten Good Laws and taught him how to lead the people? Was it not at Mount Horeb that Moses first learned the Mighty One's personal name, when He SPOKE to Moses from a burning bush? Yes, I believe they had a long and close conversation on this new mountaintop, from which Moses could view THE LAND.

I know what you're thinking. You're thinking that Moses then *marched* down that mountain and *boldly* led the people into the LAND. Nope, nada, no way! You see, Moses *died* on that mountain. That's right—Moses DIED! Were you hoping he was the special DESCENDANT of Eve? I'm sorry to say, he was not. (Although, like Enoch and Noah, he *foreshadows* him.)

STOP! Did I just say "Moses DIED"? I did, didn't I? Well, not so fast! Maybe he *died*, and maybe he *didn't die*. You see, to this *very day* no one knows where he is buried! Oh, I know that some say the Mighty One buried him, and that's very possible. But others suspect the Mighty One "took him," just as He took Enoch directly into the Mighty One's realm. Did you get that?! It's possible that Moses DIDN'T DIE, that the Mighty One simply snatched him away, as He took Enoch! If it's true, then Moses, too, ESCAPED DEATHBREATH! If so, then it is a SIGN to us of what's coming in the future, when one day—ONE DAY!—the DESCENDANT will arrive to forever DESTROY DEATH. What exactly happened to Moses on that mountaintop no one really knows. No one except the Mighty One, who once said to Moses, "My name is *I AM*."

Now that Moses is gone, who will lead this new and *faith-filled* generation of Israelites into their LAND of Promise?

Joshua will. All along, he's worked as Moses' faithful and courageous assistant. Guess what his name means? Ach! You'll never guess, so I shall tell you, and I can hardly wait. Joshua means "*I AM* saves." **CAN YOU BELIEVE THAT?!** Wow, what a name! Do not forget it, because you will see it again, and you will discover just how important it is!

Then the Mighty One **SPOKE** to Joshua: "Prepare the Israelites to cross the Jordan River into the **LAND** I am giving them. Be strong and courageous. Be careful to obey my Good Laws, meditate on them day and night, so that you will prosper. Do not be terrified, for your God, the great *I AM*, goes before you and will never forsake you." Oh . . . my . . . goodness! Some of you reading this little book are actually named **JOSHUA**. You must listen carefully to *I AM's* words to *this* Joshua. Can you hear the Mighty One speaking these same words to *you*? What's that you're saying? "My name *isn't* Joshua!" Well, neither is mine, for **PETE'S SAKE!** But I have a surprise for you: Do you trust in the Mighty One? Do you? If so, then your name *is* Joshua! Everyone who follows the Mighty One bears the name of Joshua, because it means "*I AM* saves." When you trust the Mighty One with your whole life, He (whose name is *I AM*) *saves you from evil and death*! So of course you can embrace the name Joshua as your extra, secret name.

Joshua, who was very courageous, commanded the Israelites, saying, "Get ready to move! For in *THREE DAYS* (there it is again—*three days*!) you will cross the Jordan River and enter the Land of Promise!" I believe they shouted, **"HOORAY! HOORAY!"**

THREE DAYS later, the commanders told everyone in all **TWELVE TRIBES** what to do: "When you **SEE** the golden ARK (I told you that you would get to see it!)—the one kept in the Most Holy Place in the Tabernacle—and the priests carrying it on long poles, **STAND BACK, STAND BACK!** It is too holy for you to touch! Let the golden **ARK** go in front of you, to lead you, for the great *I AM* is with it; He will go ahead of us!"

Oh, I can hear what you're saying: "This doesn't make sense. The people *never* see the **ARK**, because it's kept in the Most Holy Place where only the *high priest* sees it, and only once a year." How right you are. Except there are some things you don't yet know. When I first told you about the golden **ARK**, I did not tell you its name (it has one), nor did I tell you what treasure was stored inside it. Recall that an *ark* is a box in which treasure is stored for safekeeping. Noah's ark kept breeding pairs of all the animals, plus four pairs of "Adams and Eves" safe from the flood. Moses' tiny basket-ark kept Moses safe from the deadly waters of the River Nile. What, then, is stored so safely in *this* **ARK**—the one that sits hidden from view in the Most Holy Place? Now, at last, I can tell you: It is the two **STONE TABLETS** on which the Mighty One inscribed the Ten Good Laws—the **WORDS** He **SPOKE** to Moses at Mount Horeb! That is why the golden ark is called the **ARK OF THE COVENANT**. The Ten Good Laws formed the **COVENANT** (unbreakable promise) made between the Israelites and the Mighty One: The Israelites promised to obey His Good Laws and He promised to be their God and never, ever forsake them.

Do you also recall my telling you that the **ARK OF THE COVENANT**, in the Most Holy Place, was the Mighty One's **THRONE**? His own Presence settled over the **ARK** in a pillar of cloud and fire.

Do you see what's happening here? Joshua (whose name means . . . ?) is about to lead the people across the Jordan River and into the Land of Promise. The Mighty One, who is their God, is also their *king*; therefore, He must go before them and lead them. At His command, the priests carry His *throne*—

THIRTEEN

A NEW
GARDEN
OF DELIGHTS
(NOT!)

101

the **ARK OF THE COVENANT**—at the head of the **TWELVE TRIBES**. Not only is the **ARK** the Mighty One's *throne*, it is the *treasure chest* that holds the *Covenant*—the forever agreement between the Mighty One and the Israelites: They will obey His Words (inscribed on the stone tablets inside the ark), and He will never, ever forsake them. Goodness, did you think He would forsake them *now*, when they must face the warring Canaanites who live in the **LAND**? No, my friends, He will *never* forsake them!

So the Ark of the Covenant, carried by the priests, went *ahead* of the **TWELVE TRIBES**, and the tribes *followed* the **ARK** in their ranks of thousands.

When the priests carrying the **ARK** arrived at the Jordan, it was at flood stage. (Oh, no! **FLOOD STAGE!** Does this flood not remind you of Noah's flood—and his **ARK**?) Nevertheless, the priests waded into the waters, holding the **ARK OF THE COVENANT** *above* the flood. Immediately, the **DARK** currents parted (keep watching the *key words*), and the **WATERS** (they're like the old **SEA OF CHAOS**) piled in heaps both upstream and downstream, leaving a path of dry **GROUND** from the **EAST** side of the river to the west. Just as they had done at the Red **SEA**, the Israelites passed through the river unharmed, and all the while the Maker and Lord of the whole **EARTH**—whose Presence was with the **ARK**—stood in the Jordan until *each* and *every* beloved Israelite had crossed into the **LAND** of Promise.

They're in the **LAND**, they're in the **LAND**! After 430 years of Abraham's **DESCENDANTS** living as exiles in Egypt, plus **FORTY** years of their wandering in the wilderness, they are *home*. Imagine the **SINGING** and the **DANCING** that went on in the Israelite camp that night—their first night in the **LAND OF PROMISE!** Hopes soared. Had the Mighty One not said to them: "I, whose name is *I AM*, am bringing you into a **GOOD LAND**, a **LAND** flowing with brooks of waters,

SECRETS
of the
ANCIENT
MANUAL
REVEALED!

JOSHUA 3

DEUTERONOMY
8:7-9

fountains and depths springing out of valleys and hills, a **LAND** of wheat and barley and vines, fig trees and pomegranates, olive oil and honey, a **LAND** where you shall eat bread without any scarceness, lacking nothing." Why, one would think it was the old Garden of Delights!

Oh dear, oh dear. I must tell you something, but you're not going to like it. **WARNING: YOU'RE NOT GOING TO LIKE THIS!** The Land of Promise, though it was indeed a very *good land*, was *not* the Garden of Delights—not yet, at least—because it remained *filled* with cruel, dragon-riding Canaanites who loved the Serpent and Deathbreath and every lesser dragon too.

But in truth, the **LAND** did *not belong* to the Canaanites and *never had.* It belonged to the Mighty One, for the whole **EARTH** belongs to Him. "We will not relinquish one foot of ground!" the Canaanites growled. "This land belongs to our gods!" (Yikes!)

Slowly, the Israelites marched across the terrain, but vengeful armies opposed them, terrorizing them soul and body. But thanks be to the Mighty One, they did not fight alone. In fact, they didn't really fight at all! The gold-covered **ARK OF THE COVENANT** went before them—meaning the very Presence of the Mighty One went before them, and it was *He* who fought their battles. The Israelites needed only to stand and see the **DIVINE WARRIOR** conquer His wicked foes, freeing His **LAND** from **EVIL'S** tyranny, just as He had freed His people from Pharaoh's tyranny. (Did you *not know* that the Divine Warrior has at His command *hosts* of *unseen angelic armies*? It is true, and the Serpent and Deathbreath **COWER** before them.)

THIRTEEN

A NEW
GARDEN
OF DELIGHTS
(NOT!)

103

LIFE (AND DEATH) INSIDE THE LAND

SECRETS
of the
ANCIENT
MANUAL
REVEALED!

104

Eventually, the Mighty One took back His **LAND**, enabling the Israelites to build houses and towns, to grow crops, and to raise generations of families. Foolishly, however, they allowed numerous **DRAGON-RIDING** Canaanites to remain. It was a grave mistake, my friends, a very grave mistake. Gradually the Israelites adopted Canaanite ways, *even worshiping* their so-called gods. Why, it was the very thing the Mighty One had commanded them NOT to do: "You shall have no other 'gods' before me; make no idols."

It is heartbreaking—the things that happened after the new generation of Israelites, who were so courageous and faithful, settled in the **LAND**. You see, when they worshiped the Canaanite gods they began to behave like them. I am loath (extremely hesitant, unwilling) to describe their behaviors, but I must, for I have sworn to tell you the truth about the world. The Israelites grew petty-minded and self-centered; they craved riches and power. *Riches? Power?* Are the Israelites not the Mighty One's children? Everything that exists belongs to Him. Why, then, do they need *riches?* And do they not belong to the only good and true Divine Warrior, who commands hosts of unseen angelic armies to defeat evil? Why, then, do they need *power?* Do you see what's happened? The once faithful, dragon-defying Israelites have now joined forces with the **SERPENT** and become **DRAGON RIDERS.** Oh, their practices are so loathsome (see the glossary) I can barely speak of them!

Can you guess what else they did? They ignored (I repeat: **IGNORED**) the widows, orphans, and alien foreigners in their midst! The Mighty One *loves* the poor and the outcasts, yet the Israelites treated them as less than animals. Their flocks and herds ate their fill, while the poor starved.

You can well imagine that the Israelites also ignored the Mighty One, even scoffed at Him, saying things such as, "Ha! Who is the Mighty One? Who is the great *I AM?* He cannot see us or hear us!" Of course, it was their so-called gods that could not see or hear, for they were only wood and stone. So far did they go in wandering from the Mighty One, the wayward Israelites sometimes—sometimes!—sacrificed their own children to the awful gods. **EXCUSE ME?!** Did they not remember the story of their ancestor Abraham and his son Isaac? How the Mighty One commanded Abraham to **NOT HARM THE BOY?** Have they forgotten their *Covenant* with the Mighty One, the forever agreement they made to obey His Ten Good Laws? Have they forgotten the Law that says, **"NO MURDER"?** Have they forgotten that the stone tablets on which the Mighty One inscribed the Ten Laws are stored and safeguarded in the **ARK OF THE COVENANT** inside the Most Holy Place?

Oh yes, they have indeed **FORGOTTEN!**

The levels of lawlessness, greed, and injustice in the **LAND** of Promise became nearly intolerable, much like in the days of Noah before the flood and the Great Rescue.

I can hear what you're saying. You're saying, "With evil being **EVERY-WHERE**—[hey, you don't have to shout!]—why doesn't the Mighty One come down and end the evil all at once?"

My friend, it is not that simple, not that simple at all! As I explained earlier, the **SERPENT'S EVIL** had entered the **SOIL-CREATURES** like a virulent (powerfully poisonous) infection that invaded every part of them (and us). It's not that they were no longer **GOOD**, or beautiful, bearing the Mighty One's **IMAGE**, but that **IMAGE** was marred (damaged), because their beauty and **GOODNESS** were always *mixed* with ugly **EVIL**. To cut it out of a person would be to kill the patient! No,

THIRTEEN

A NEW
GARDEN
OF DELIGHTS
(NOT!)

105

no, that would never do; the Mighty One loves His CREATURES too much to do such a thing!

There was only one solution: the SERPENT and Deathbreath must be fought (the horror!) and DEFEATED. Then the SOIL-CREATURES must be re-made, with new SOIL-CREATURE bodies, completely cleansed of the EVIL SERPENT'S insidious (stealthy and creeping) infection. But who *would*—or *could*—do such a thing? I'M NOT TELLING YOU (yet).

CHAPTER FOURTEEN

JUDGES AND GIANTS

From THE BOOKS CALLED JUDGES, SAMUEL,
KINGS, *and* CHRONICLES

JUDGES,
SAMUEL, KINGS,
AND CHRONICLES

D ID I NOT SWEAR TO TELL YOU THE TRUTH about the world? I did, and I shall. Now you have seen just how much the Land of Promise was *not* the new Garden of Delights. Far from it! The Israelites forgot their *Covenant* with the Mighty One, their forever promise to obey His Good Laws. Is it not obvious, Dragon Slayer, that when a person rejects the Good Laws there is nothing but *lawlessness?*

To keep the evil (yes, please do keep watching for *key words*) somewhat in check, the Mighty One gave the Israelites judges and kings to rule over them, to put the brakes on murder, lying, thieving, and such like. First came a long series of judges, brave men—and one woman—who attempted to rule the now dragon-riding Israelites. What was life like in the Land of Promise during this lawless era? Why, it was like the wild, wild West—only **WORSE!** Everyone did *exactly* what he or she wanted to do, no matter how bad it was. Imagine your school with *no* teachers, *no* leaders, *no one* who cares a lick about anyone else, and *no rules at all.* (I shudder.) *Never* would I step inside such a place, *never!*

The judges sent by the Mighty One were, in fact, mighty warriors, and lest you think theirs was a simple task, think again: You see, by the time each new judge came on the scene, the Israelites had committed such grave evils they cowered in fear in caves, because their enemies *hunted* and *enslaved* them. **CAN YOU BELIEVE IT**? Once again they were *slaves—slaves* in their *own land.* Once they reached that point—which they did, over and over again—then a warrior-judge would rise to power to defeat the enemy, free the Israelites, and establish peace once again in the **LAND** of Promise.

But not for long. **NOT FOR LONG!** After peace was established, what monstrous creep do you think slithered into the towns and villages of the Land of Promise? Could it be . . . the **SEA SERPENT**?! Yes! That Father of Lies, that hater of all goodness, crept into every house and marketplace, disguising itself as a thing of beauty. The horror! It whispered into the minds and hearts of the Israelites, "Look at the Canaanite and Philistine gods. They provide the sun and rain, they give you all your crops. They control everything in your lives. Bow down to them! Worship them, so they will not harm you! If you bow before them, you too will be gods!"

Sound familiar? Like their ancestors in the Garden of Delights, Abraham's **DESCENDANTS** *believed* the bilious Serpent. Oh, they became "gods" all right, for when they worshiped these so-called gods of their enemies, they became like them: They lied, cheated, and stole; they robbed the poor; they broke their promises to each other and sometimes murdered their own children! That's when their enemies conquered and enslaved them. (Well, of course they did! How could the Mighty One protect them when they ceased *trusting Him*, when they *shook their fists at Him*, and said, "We care nothing about the Mighty One!"?)

Not until they grew really, really desperate did they return to the Mighty One, crying, "Help us! Save us!" And every single time they cried to Him, the Mighty One sent a warrior-judge to defeat their enemies and bring peace.

It became an ugly **PATTERN:** Evil, slavery, a cry for help, a warrior-judge, the enemy defeated, peace established; evil, slavery, a cry for help, a warrior-judge, the enemy defeated, peace established; evil, slavery . . . on and on it went.

I can hear what you're saying. You're saying, **"WHY** did the Mighty One keep delivering them? Why didn't He just **LEAVE THOSE UNGRATEFUL PEOPLE IN THE DUST?!"**

All I can say is, **"I DON'T KNOW!"**

WAIT! I *do* know, I really *do*. If you've been paying attention, you already know, too. *O the Mighty One, merciful and compassionate, slow to anger and abounding in lovingkindness.* (It comes straight from the *Ancient Manual*.) That is why, when they cried to Him, He always answered His wayward people and *saved them*. He did it because He **LOVES THEM.** Even though they forgot their forever promise to obey His Good Laws, He never forgot His forever promise to *not forsake them*.

EXODUS 34:6

A KING IS CROWNED

After a long series of warrior-judges (those stories are truly wild, but I cannot retell them here—perhaps in another book), the Mighty One gave His people a *king*. For years they had cried to Him, "Give us a king! Give us a king!" And He had answered, "I am your king! You need no other!" But the people insisted—nay, **DEMANDED!** Do you know *why* they demanded a soil-creature king? It was for an awful reason, truly awful. It was because they *wanted to be like the other nations.* **EXCUSE ME?!** Was it not through *them*, Abraham's **DESCENDANTS**, that the Mighty One would **BLESS** all the nations? Was it not through *them* that the Mighty One would *save* all the nations? Abraham's **DESCENDANTS** were called to show the whole world who the Mighty One is! And what life looks like when soil-creatures obey the Mighty One as their true, only, and good *king*.

Dear reader, see what trouble we can get into when we make it our chief goal to *be like other soil-creatures*, rather than striving to obey and worship the Mighty One. How often I've done it myself. It is pure foolishness, I tell you, **FOOLISHNESS**.

The Mighty One gave his people a **SOIL-CREATURE** king (many, many kings, in fact, over hundreds of years), but oh the trouble it caused! You see, a **SOIL-CREATURE** king will always (I repeat: **ALWAYS**) be tempted by the **SERPENT**, and will always cave in. He or she will, at some point, do **EVIL**.

Their first king was Saul. He was tall and handsome. The Philistines who, along with the Canaanites, inhabited the Land of Promise, went to war against Saul. The Philistine warriors formed a battle line on the hill they occupied, while the Israelite warriors formed an opposing battle line on the hill they

SECRETS
of the
ANCIENT
MANUAL
REVEALED!

110

occupied. In between the two armies lay a long valley. From the Philistine ranks a giant of a man stepped forward: Goliath. He shouted to the Israelites, "I defy King Saul and the entire Israelite army! Send out a man to fight me! If I win, the victory is for the Philistines. If your man wins, the victory is for the Israelites."

Just thinking about Goliath makes me tremble! And I can tell you, when they heard Goliath's shouts, King Saul and all the Israelite warriors quaked in fear too. Goliath was over nine feet tall. He wore a bronze helmet and a bronze coat of armor that weighed **125 POUNDS!** His shins were covered with bronze plates; he carried a bronze javelin; and his spear had an iron point that weighed 15 pounds. It was hopeless. No Israelite warrior could possibly fight and defeat such a giant.

For *FORTY* days—**FORTY DAYS!** Wow, it's as if the Israelites are in the destroying flood in Noah's time, facing certain *death*—Goliath appeared every morning and every evening, standing in the valley between the two armies, shouting, "I defy the Israelite army! Send someone to fight me!" But no one from Israel dared to approach him.

Until a young lad named David arrived. The son of Jesse, from the little town of Bethlehem in Judea (not far from Jerusalem), David visited the battleground to bring food to his brothers, who were warriors. (You may be asking, What is Judea? Why, it is the land belonging to Judah—one of the **TWELVE TRIBES** of Israel.) David heard Goliath shouting, "Send a man to fight me!" and he saw the Israelite warriors run in terror. Being young, he was only a shepherd boy, and his brothers did not want him at the battleground. They quarreled, as brothers often do. "Why are you here?" his brothers demanded. "Go home and tend the sheep! You're just a conceited little kid—now, scram!"

David answered, "*Now* what have I said? Good grief, am I not allowed to open my mouth?"

What David had said was this: "Who is this godless Philistine that he should defy the armies of the Mighty One, the God of Life?!"

Young David ventured into the presence of King Saul himself and told the king that he, David, would fight Goliath. "What?!" Saul exclaimed. "Why, you're only a boy!" David answered, "True, I am young, and only a shepherd, but I have killed lions and bears to save my sheep. The Mighty One, whose name is *I AM*, saved me from the lion and the bear, and He will save me from this godless Philistine who dares to defy the One True God!"

King Saul believed David. He dressed David in his own armor, but it was too big for David and cumbersome (heavy and clumsy). "I cannot move in this massive armor," David said. Then he took it off, grabbed his staff, and went to the nearby stream. He chose five smooth stones from the water and put them in his shepherd's bag. Taking his slingshot in his hand, he deliberately began walking . . . across . . . the valley . . . that lay between the two opposing armies.

Goliath moved closer, his shield bearer carrying a mammoth shield in front of the giant. When he got close enough to see that David was only a boy, he roared with disgust. "Do you think I am only a little dog?! Are you going to beat me up with your sticks?! By all the gods of the Philistines, I curse you—you little rat! Come here, so I can cut you into pieces and feed your flesh to the birds and beasts!"

David did not flinch. He knew the gods of the Philistines were *nothing*— nothing but wood and stone. He shouted to Goliath, "You think you can come against me with your sword, your spear, and your javelin. But I come against *you* in the name of *I AM*, the Almighty, whose army you defy! This day the great *I AM* will give you into my hand and I will defeat you and cut off your head! Then *I* will feed *your* flesh to the birds and the beasts, and the whole world will know that the Mighty One, whose name is *I AM*, is God in Israel! The battle belongs to Him, and it is not by swords or spears that He saves, but by His own might!"

Goliath and his shield bearer moved closer to David, and suddenly David ran toward the giant, as fast as his legs could carry him. He took a stone from his bag, put it into his sling, whirled the weapon with all his might and released the deadly, speeding stone. It struck Goliath in the center of his forehead, sinking deep into his skull, and he fell flat on his face. Seizing the giant's sword, David killed that godless Philistine and cut off his head. Struck with terror, the Philistine army fled from the Israelites, and the Mighty One triumphed that day, through the courage and trust of a young boy with a slingshot and a single stone.

King Saul was jealous—very jealous—and he soon set his heart to kill David, especially because the Mighty One **SPOKE** to the prophet Samuel, saying that He, the Mighty One, was taking the throne from Saul and his offspring and giving it to David and his offspring. So Samuel anointed David as Israel's second king; but for the years before Saul's death, David ran from Saul, hiding in caves with his band of brave men, for Saul hunted him as if David were a wild animal.

David became not only Israel's second but also her *greatest* king, for he was a man after the Mighty One's own heart. He **LOVED** the Mighty One! He called Him by name, *I AM*, and he longed to obey His Ten Good Laws.

David, strong warrior-king, conquered the Jebusite city of Jerusalem, making it the capital of the **TWELVE TRIBES**. He also brought the Tabernacle to Jerusalem, permanently! Yes, the **TABERNACLE**, the Mighty One's own tent, His portable Temple, where the golden **ARK OF THE COVENANT** sat in the Most Holy Place. The **ARK** was the Mighty One's throne, for His Presence settled above it in a pillar of cloud and fire.

HOW THE MIGHTY ARE FALLEN!

Are you wondering if David is the special **DESCENDANT** of **EVE**, who will one day—**ONE DAY!**—arrive to **CRUSH** the **SERPENT'S** head and destroy Deathbreath? Well, are you? It's a good guess, but it is not correct. Although, like Enoch, and Noah, and Moses, and Joshua, and many others, David definitely *foreshadows* the special **DESCENDANT**, **HE IS NOT THE ONE**. But we're getting closer to the **DESCENDANT**, yes we are, because David *foreshadows* him more than anyone else. As I said, he loved the Mighty One with all his heart; nevertheless (I'm very sorry to have to tell you this), he failed miserably in keeping the Ten Laws. David loved beautiful women; it was his great weakness. Despite the Mighty One's command to him, and to all Israel's kings, to *not* take extra wives, as their enemies always did, David disobeyed. He had **LOTS AND LOTS** of **WIVES!**

II SAMUEL 11

Oh dear, this was a very bad situation. But it got even worse. Ach! He *coveted* another man's wife and then secretly arranged to have the husband killed in battle! Oh, it was awful, just awful, and David knew it. Why, it was murder, it was! When he finally came to his senses and saw the evils he had committed (adultery *and* murder!), his heart filled with bitter remorse. He prayed to the Mighty One, saying, "O God of All, against you, and you only have I sinned and

PSALM 51

done what is *evil* in your sight. My sins are always in front of me. Have mercy on me, for your love is unfailing and your compassion is great. Make my heart clean and pure again, and do not cast me away from your Presence."

I'm happy to report that the Mighty One, who is rich in mercy, *did* create a new and clean heart inside David. And David worshiped and praised the great *I AM* for the rest of his days on **EARTH**. Do not (I repeat: **DO NOT**) forget David's name! It is *extremely important* as you will soon come to see. Practice it now: King David, King David, King David! And please do **NOT** forget where David grew up: the little town of Bethlehem, in the Land of Judea.

When David died, his son Solomon reigned in his place. The Mighty One granted Solomon wisdom and the skills to manage large building projects. It was Solomon who replaced the portable Tabernacle/Temple (which David had placed in Jerusalem) with a *permanent* house for the Mighty One. He built a splendid Temple on the mountaintop at the center of Jerusalem, and some say this is the *very mountaintop* to which Abraham took a **THREE-DAY** journey with Isaac. It was on this *very mountaintop* that the Mighty One called to him, "Abraham! Put away the knife! Do not harm the boy!" It was on this *very mountaintop* that the Mighty One provided a ram to sacrifice in place of Abraham's son. Yes, that is the mountaintop on which Solomon built a magnificent Temple for the sacred Presence. And the Presence of the great *I AM* was pleased to dwell there, and His glory **FILLED** the Temple that Solomon built in the center of Jerusalem, in the center of the Israelite nation, in the center of the **LAND**, in the center of the world.

CHAPTER FIFTEEN

THE VOICE OF THE GREAT *I AM*

From BOOKS IN THE LATTER HALF OF THE
AGREEMENT ANTĪQUÁTUS

AGREEMENT
ANTĪQUÁTUS

KING SOLOMON, DESPITE ALL HIS WISDOM, riches, and glory . . . died. Well, of course he did! Deathbreath takes everyone! (Except for Enoch—and maybe Moses—and someone else, too—wait and see!) Solomon's son Rehoboam inherited the throne. He was the grandson of the great King David (whose name you are remembering, right?), but his heart was as DARK as the DARK SEA of Chaos. He was nothing more than a vengeful dragon rider (I repeat: REHOBOAM WAS A DRAGON RIDER!) and one of the worst ever. He was no better than the tyrant pharaohs of Egypt who had enslaved his ancestors. I am sorry to tell you that he was only the *first* in a long, long series of wicked idol-worshiping, dragon-riding monarchs in the **LAND** of Promise who led the Israelites far, far away from the **COVENANT** their ancestors had made with the Mighty One at Mount Horeb, when He gave them the Ten Laws and they promised to **OBEY** every one of His **WORDS**. Ach! In reality, they did everything BUT obey the Mighty One. They did all the things He abhors: they cheated the poor; they lied in court; their judges ruled unfairly; they coveted their neighbors' stuff—including their neighbors' spouses; they stole and they murdered; they even sacrificed their own children to the so-called gods. Oh, it was **HORRIBLE!** It was as if they had never heard the Mighty One **SPEAK** at all. (I know this is beginning to sound like the same story over and over again, but it's **TRUE**. Over and over, the Mighty One's chosen people committed unspeakable *wrongs*. They were no different from the rest of us!)

I don't know about you, but if I were the Mighty One (and it's a good thing I'm not), I think I would never **SPEAK** again to these hard-hearted people. But **SPEAK** He did—not directly, as He had to Moses—but through brave Dragon Slayers called prophets (people specially chosen by the Mighty One to **SPEAK** *on His behalf*). Here's how it worked: The Mighty One **SPOKE** to the prophets, and the prophets then **SPOKE** His **WORDS** to the people. The Mighty One said to the prophets, "I am the God of your ancestors, whose secret name is *I AM*. Say to my people, '*I AM* says: Turn from your wicked ways! Forsake your idols! Return to the One True God and He will pardon you and rescue you from your bondage to evil!'" The prophets, because they were faithful Dragon Slayers, then repeated the Mighty One's **WORDS** to the people. Theirs was *not* an easy task. Do you think the people *wanted* to hear the Mighty One's **WORDS**? They did not! They put their hands over their ears and shouted "La-la-la-la-la—we can't hear you!"

Can you guess what else the people said to the prophets? Basically, it was something like **SHUT UP!** Oh, they scorned the prophets, sometimes even murdered them. They **MURDERED** them—those who delivered the very **WORDS** of the great *I AM!*

SURPRISE FACT: I can tell you truly that one prophet, named Elijah, was clearly *not* murdered. How do I know that, you ask? I know that because the *Ancient Manual* tells us that Elijah *did not die*. That's right, he **DID NOT DIE!** (If he did not die, then he could not have been murdered.) This is difficult to believe, but it's true: Elijah was "taken" by the Mighty One. To be more specific, he was taken up in a whirlwind into the Mighty One's realm. Like Enoch, and possibly Moses, he is a sign to us that Deathbreath will one day be defeated!

Well, as I was saying, the Israelites mostly told the prophets to **SHUT UP.** Nevertheless, the Mighty One, because He had sworn in a **COVENANT** to never, ever leave His people, **SPOKE** again (and again and again) through the prophets, saying, "I will restore the throne of *King David*. I will raise up a **DESCENDANT** from his line, born in *Bethlehem*, David's hometown, and he will rule in justice, righteousness, and peace."

Did I not tell you that soon you would discover the importance of King David?! Here it is, here it is! The Mighty One *promised*, speaking through His prophets, that one day—**ONE DAY!**—He would send a *new* "King David," one of David's own **DESCENDANTS**, to rescue His people from all their enemies. Wow!

Unfortunately, very few of the Israelites *listened* to the voice of *I AM*, although I'm happy to say some did. Some were true Dragon Slayers, and they waited for the DESCENDANT of King David to arrive. No one knew when this "new David" would appear, but those who trusted the Mighty One waited and watched for him. They called him the Messiah (it means "anointed one"), and they trusted that one day—ONE DAY!—he would set up his kingdom of goodness, truth, and love, driving out all the wicked tyrants. He was their hope. But few believed. Most were interested only in dragonish ways and deeds.

WELL, speaking of dragonish ways: In the kingdom of Assyria, far to the EAST of the LAND of Promise, the dragons reveled in festivals of greed and hate and violent wars. Haughty Assyrian kings WELCOMED the brutes, fed them, and rode upon their backs for sport. "YIPPEEE!" the dragons shrieked deliriously when Assyrian warriors rode them westward, to the LAND OF PROMISE, where, drunk on dragon drool, brutal Assyrians viciously conquered the ten northernmost tribes of Israel—who were never heard from again. Oh . . . my . . . goodness! Ten of the TWELVE TRIBES are now *gone*—GONE!

The two southern tribes (Judah and Benjamin, who called themselves the Kingdom of Judah, whose people called themselves the *Jews*) were all that was left of Abraham's uncountable DESCENDANTS. They struggled on, hoping against hope that the Assyrians would not destroy them as well. They needn't have worried, because another power, greater even than Assyria, marched against Judah: Babylon. BABYLON! Oh, the weeping and wailing when Babylon's warriors invaded Jerusalem, Judah's capital. They burned everything and toppled the city walls; and worst of all (I hate to tell you this, but I must), they demolished King Solomon's beautiful Temple to the Mighty One, whose name is *I AM*. When the Babylonian warriors had finished their siege, the Temple stood in *ruins*. The Temple! Where the Mighty One's glory dwelt! Where the Mighty One's Presence had so long remained above the ARK OF THE COVENANT in the Most Holy Place! Not since Abraham's descendants had lived as slaves in Egypt had anything *so awful* happened!

Taking the Jews who survived, the Babylonians marched them, broken and humiliated, *eastward* to Babylon (just as Adam and Eve had gone *eastward* when they were driven from the Garden of Delights), where the Jews lived in exile for seventy long years. Why, it was something like being back in Egypt. For there they were in Babylon, separated from their LAND, separated from their Temple, living among false so-called gods. I detect the stink of the old SEA, don't you? PEEE-YEW! Now there is chaos and DARKNESS, loneliness and fear, dragons and more dragons.

Exiled in faraway Babylon where no one knew the Mighty One and His GOODNESS, the Jews dreamed of Jerusalem, and their Temple, and the Presence of their great *I AM*. They remembered all the Mighty One's WORDS SPOKEN through the prophets and they grieved the EVILS they had committed. Try to imagine how they felt: Over and over, they could still hear the prophets' WORDS haunting their minds—all the WORDS they had IGNORED. The worst of it was, they remembered (how could they forget?) that they had MURDERED the prophets! They had MURDERED the very people the Mighty One had sent to *rescue them.* Oh, it was so DREADFUL I cannot bear to think of it.

Question: What two BLESSINGS had the Mighty One promised Abraham?

Answer: *Land* and *descendants.*

Question: How many descendants would Abraham have?

Answer: Like the STARS in the night sky, there would be *too many to count.*

SECRETS
of the
ANCIENT
MANUAL
REVEALED!

120

FACT TO RECALL: The Jews exiled in Babylon were now the *only remnant left* of Abraham's uncountable descendants.

CAN YOU BELIEVE IT?! Ten of the **TWELVE TRIBES** are *gone*, and the remaining two tribes, Judah and Benjamin, are now *separated from their* **LAND**, and . . . well, there are so few of them! They had *not* (I repeat: they had **NOT**) fulfilled their **COVENANT** (forever promise) with the Mighty One, in which they promised to keep His Good Laws and He promised to never leave them. The **COVENANT** was *broken*, I tell you, *broken—by them!* Ah, but the Mighty One—*O the Mighty One, merciful and gracious, slow to anger, abounding in lovingkindness*—had not forgotten *His* side of the **COVENANT**, *His* promise to never, ever forsake them. He heard their cries in Babylon, and He set about to rescue His people once more. (I'm so excited I can barely write, but I must tell you to watch carefully, because the Mighty One, the One True God of all the Earth, is about to use soil-creatures who do not even *know* Him to do His **GOOD** work!)

It was the Persians who defeated the Babylonians, and the new king of Persia, because he **HEARD THE VOICE OF THE MIGHTY ONE COMMANDING HIM TO DO THIS**, permitted the Jews to return to their **LAND**—to Jerusalem—to rebuild Solomon's ruined Temple to the Mighty One. Did you get that? The Jews are going home and they're going to *rebuild the Temple!* I'm getting goosebumps!

Try to remember that the Jews have been in exile for *seventy years*. It's been a long time since they've seen Jerusalem. They've traveled a very long distance to get back there, and all the while they've been singing and imagining the thrill of seeing the old City once again. Can you *feel* their devastating disappointment when they first lay eyes on their once beautiful Jerusalem and

FIFTEEN

THE VOICE
OF THE
GREAT *I AM*

EXODUS 34:6

121

the Mighty One's once beautiful Temple? Dragon Slayers, I must tell you: They threw themselves down and wept. (I am not ashamed to admit that I, too, am weeping.)

SECRETS
of the
ANCIENT
MANUAL
REVEALED!

122

The Jews did not feel strong. The current inhabitants of the **LAND** (yes, yes, I've been underlining, because I fear you've forgotten your **ASSIGNMENT**— please do carry on with your work) were much like the Canaanites their ancestors had failed to drive out: They knew not the Mighty One and they wanted to crush the Jews (I repeat: they wanted to **CRUSH** the Jews!). Taunting the returned exiles, the inhabitants of the **LAND** made life very hard for them. But the Mighty One was with His people and slowly, gradually, they rebuilt the Temple and their lives.

They began with the altar, rebuilding it with stones, and they offered whole burnt offerings upon it, morning and evening, declaring their whole-hearted obedience to the Mighty One. They even celebrated the Feast of Tabernacles! Why, they hadn't celebrated any of their sacred festivals for **SEVENTY YEARS!** Anyone younger than seventy years old had **NEVER** celebrated it! Do you know what the Feast of Tabernacles *is*? Why, it is the Jews' greatest festival of all, their fall harvest festival, the one the Mighty One commanded them to observe every year. For eight days and nights, they lived in little huts, remembering that for **FORTY YEARS** their ancestors had lived in tents as they wandered in the wilderness. They remembered that never, in **FORTY YEARS**, had the Mighty One forsaken them and let them go without food and water. Now, for eight days, they danced and sang and gave thanks to the Mighty One for all of His provisions.

Guess what else they did at the Feast of Tabernacles? You'll never guess, so I'll just tell you. They *prayed* for the arrival of the **MESSIAH**, the new "King

David" who would come to save them from their enemies, forever. Oh, what joy it was to celebrate the Feast of Tabernacles once again!

After the rebuilding of the altar, the returned exiles began repairing the Temple's walls. Oh . . . my . . . goodness, it was such a frightening time! Every day they worked in dread, because the inhabitants of the land threatened to drive them out—or kill them. But the Mighty One protected them. Their stonemasons dressed the newly quarried stones, and their carpenters imported cedar logs from Lebanon, and no one stopped them. CAN YOU BELIEVE IT?! Just like when they marched out of Egypt on that night so long ago, NO ONE STOPPED THEM!

When the Temple's foundations were finally laid, the priests put on their vestments, the trumpeters blew their trumpets, the musicians clapped their loud cymbals, and the people SHOUTED with joy to the Mighty One! They sang, with the singers leading them:

The Mighty One is good,

His love endures forever!

Joy filled the streets, but the older Israelites—how my heart aches for them!—the ones old enough to have seen King Solomon's glorious Temple before the Babylonians destroyed it, sat down and wept. There were shouts of joy and wails of grief, and no one could tell which was which because there was SO MUCH NOISE.

Reader, are you not AMAZED by what the Mighty One has done for this tiny remnant of Abraham's once countless DESCENDANTS? They are back in their own LAND, they are restoring the Mighty One's Temple, and they are waiting for the MESSIAH. There's something I haven't yet told you. A man named Ezra, a priest and teacher who had returned to Jerusalem from exile in Babylon, had

EZRA 3:11

SECRETS
of the
ANCIENT
MANUAL
REVEALED!

124

in his possession a scroll on which were written all the Good Laws the Mighty One had given their ancestors at Mount Horeb, and all the instructions the Mighty One had spoken to Moses. Oh . . . my . . . goodness! The Jews had not been studying the Mighty One's Words for over seventy years! Now they longed for His Words like thirsty travelers in the desert longed for water. (I hope you do, too; I really hope you do, too!) The carpenters built a high platform, then Ezra stood upon it, so everyone could see him and hear his words, and he read aloud from the precious scroll. When the people heard the beautiful Words from their great *I AM*, they wept for joy. They wept, and wept, and wept.

My goodness, there's a lot of weeping going on, isn't there? Well, wouldn't *you* weep if you had been driven from your home, and your place of worship, for SEVENTY YEARS?!

"Where is our promised Messiah?" they said to one another. "Where is the new 'King David' who will one day—ONE DAY!—defeat our oppressors, forever saving us from slavery and exile, the one who will establish the Mighty One's kingdom *here on Earth*, a kingdom of peace and true justice, love and goodness, and rest."

And so, back in their good land they waited, for they had no idea when their Messiah would arrive.

So ends the record from Epeisódion One: the *Agreement Antīquắtus.*

THE DESCENDANTS OF ABRAHAM
LEADING TO THE SPECIAL
DESCENDANT OF EVE

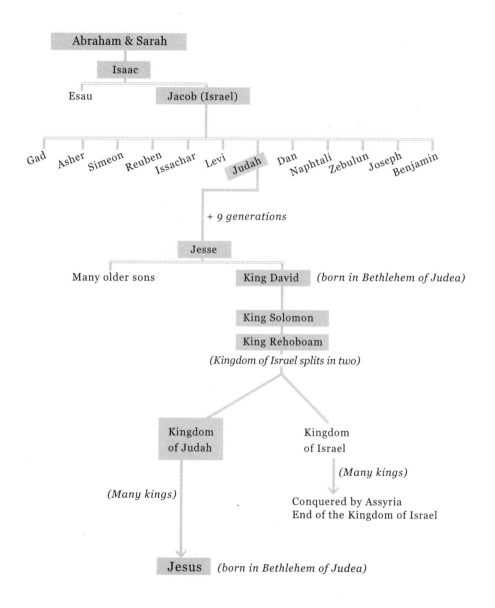

Abraham & Sarah

Isaac

Esau   Jacob (Israel)

Gad   Asher   Simeon   Reuben   Issachar   Levi   Judah   Dan   Naphtali   Zebulun   Joseph   Benjamin

+ 9 generations

Jesse

Many older sons   King David   *(born in Bethlehem of Judea)*

King Solomon

King Rehoboam

(Kingdom of Israel splits in two)

Kingdom of Judah   Kingdom of Israel

(Many kings)

(Many kings)   Conquered by Assyria
End of the Kingdom of Israel

Jesus   *(born in Bethlehem of Judea)*

EPEISÓDION ZERO
(This is not out of order—you'll see)

THE SILENCE

Let me explain.

Hundreds of years lie between Epeisódion One and Epeisódion Two of the *Ancient Manual*. During this long period, the Jews hear nothing (**NOTHING**) from the Mighty One. The events of these years are *not* described in the *Ancient Manual*, but I, Sir Wyvern Pugilist, thanks to my intense studies in world history, can tell you something about them.

Time passed, and new powers marched across the world's stage. The Greeks, under their young and maniacal leader Alexander the Great, conquered **EVERYTHING** in their path. With their philosophical ideas, the Greeks ruled a large part of the world, but they did not make it better, no they did **NOT**. The world remained a harsh and dangerous place, full of murder, greed, and the lust for power.

The Jews waited for their Messiah.

Next came the Romans, so mathematical, such great engineers. They built massive aqueducts to deliver water to cities (they invented the first sewage system, complete with flush toilets!); they built roads that connected every far-flung country to every other far-flung country. Brutal, cold-hearted killing machines were their warriors. Where the Greeks had once ruled, the Romans supplanted (replaced) them. Their empire spread and spread. There was a new sense of "peace" on Earth, but not the peace that drives out fear. This so-called peace was *based* on fear—fear of the dungeon, fear of the Roman executioners.

In the Land of Promise, as in most of the world, Roman soldiers kept watch at every city gate, and Roman prisons filled up with the likes of anyone who dared to oppose Caesar (the title given to Roman emperors).

More than ever, the Jews longed for their Messiah to appear, to free them from the Roman oppressors and to cleanse their land of pagan Roman idols.

Hundreds of years had passed since their return from Babylon and the painstaking reconstruction of their ruined Temple; and in that time no one had heard **ONE SINGLE WORD** from the Mighty One. No prophets had spoken. No mountains had quaked and smoked. No bushes had burned with unconsuming flames. After enduring centuries of this awful silence, the Jews despaired of ever being free again.

Rebel insurgents often claimed to be the Messiah, promising that they and their roughneck gangs would defeat Rome. But these big-talking resistance fighters were only that—big talkers. And they stirred up more trouble. Every time one of them came rabble-rousing through the streets of Jerusalem, Rome only tightened its control and silenced these blusterers—permanently (if you know what I mean).

Hope was in short supply.

Had the great *I AM* abandoned the Jews forever?

THE AGREEMENT
NOVUS
UN-PARALLELUS

132

Let me explain.

The *Ancient Manual* (yes, I know, some folks call it the Bible, but I use its true title) is divided into two parts: Epeisódion One: *The Agreement Antīquắtus* and Epeisódion Two: *The Agreement Novus Un-Parallelus*. The second part (the *Agreement Novus Un-Parallelus*) is much, much smaller than the first part. It begins with events that happened over two thousand years ago in King David's city—the little town of Bethlehem, in the Land of Judea. To understand what I mean by the *Agreement Novus Un-Parallelus*, you'll need to keep reading.

CHAPTER ONE

ANGELS AND KINGS

From THE BOOKS BY LUKE *and* MATTHEW

WARNING: Just because we're now in *The Agreement Novus Un-Paralellus* does **NOT** mean you can slack off watching for *key words* to appear. No, no! Be ever vigilant!

LUKE AND
MATTHEW

AFTER HUNDREDS OF YEARS OF SILENCE, the Mighty One—at last!—**SPOKE** to the Jews, the remnant of Abraham's countless descendants. Phew! Were you beginning to think He would never speak again? Me too. Here's how it happened:

While Rome ruled the world, and Herod the Great was king over the ancient Land of Promise, the angel Gabriel (it means "God is my hero") appeared to a

girl in the insignificant, meager town of Nazareth. The girl's name was Mary, and perhaps you've heard of her. She was a virgin, engaged to a good man named Joseph, of the House of David, but they would not share a bed until they were fully married.

Out of nowhere it seemed, the angel Gabriel just . . . **APPEARED**, and said, "Greetings, Mary! You are highly favored, for the Mighty One is with you." You can imagine her terror, but Gabriel said, "Fear not! You will bear a child, the son of the Mighty One."

"But how can that happen," she wondered aloud, "since I have never slept with a man."

Gabriel said, "The Most High will overshadow you and you will become pregnant with a son by the Holy Spirit. You must name him Jesus. He will be great, the Son of the Most High. The Mighty One will give to Him the throne of His ancestor **KING DAVID,** and His kingdom will be forever. For with the Mighty One, nothing is impossible."

Bursting with joy and wonder, Mary proclaimed, "I am the Mighty One's servant! Let it be done to me according to His purpose."

OH . . . MY . . . GOODNESS! Mary's son will inherit the throne of His ancestor **KING DAVID?!** Could it . . . is it . . . is it really coming true?! Mary's son is—oh, my!— He's the—the promised king, from *David's descendants*. He is the **MESSIAH!**

When Joseph learned that Mary was pregnant, he was utterly humiliated, and he didn't want to marry her, because (of course) he believed her baby came from another man. But the angel visited Joseph and said to him, "Do not hesitate to take Mary as your wife, for the baby in her womb is from the Holy Spirit. You must name Him Jesus for He will save his people from their sins." So Joseph—who was such a good man and who deeply loved the Mighty

One—married her, even though most of the people in Nazareth believed Mary had been unfaithful to him, and I'm sure they persecuted her for it. And Mary and Joseph, who could not have been more courageous, waited expectantly for their miracle baby to arrive. Now, after this—

STOP, STOP, STOP!

Question: After Moses' death, who led the Israelites into the Land of Promise? (Hint: He was a strong commander of armies.)

Answer: You're right—it was Joshua.

Question: What does the name Joshua mean? What's that? You say you can't remember? Reader, you must, you must! It's extremely important! Oh, very well, instead of going back umpteen chapters to find it, I shall simply tell you. Joshua means "*I AM* saves."

IMPORTANT INFORMATION: The name Jesus is simply a Greek form of the Hebrew name Joshua. In other words, Jesus has Joshua's name! Therefore, Jesus means "*I AM* saves." That is why Gabriel said, "Name him *Jesus*—because He will *save his people* from their sins." It's so **AMAZING!** Through *Joshua,* the great *I AM* saved the Israelites from their enemies the Canaanites. But *Jesus* will save them from far greater enemies: He will save them from their *sins.* That means He will save them from their bondage to the evil **SEA SERPENT**, for it is the **SERPENT** that tempts them to sin, and it is sin that opens the gates to Deathbreath. And not only that, Jesus will save the *whole world* from its sins, for the **SERPENT** has tempted *all* **SOIL-CREATURES** to do things that harm the Creation, that oppose **LIFE** and love and **GOODNESS**.

Oh, I can hear what you're asking: "If Jesus is the new 'King David,' their Messiah who will rescue the Jews from their oppressors, is He also the special DESCENDANT of EVE who will one day—ONE DAY!—arrive to CRUSH the Serpent's head?" Well, what do you think? (I can tell you this much, Jesus *is* a DESCENDANT of Eve. But we're getting ahead of the story.)

About the same time the angel Gabriel visited Mary, the Roman emperor

LUKE 2:1-3

Caesar Augustus issued a decree: *Every person in my empire must be counted. Return to your home city, every man of you, with his wife and children, to register for the census.*

136

Joseph saddled his donkey and took Mary, who was very pregnant, and they traveled south to Bethlehem, David's hometown, because Joseph belonged to the DESCENDANTS of King David. (Oh, I do hope you're watching, as I am, for all of the *key words*.)

In Bethlehem, everyone's guest rooms were full, so Mary and Joseph sheltered with a peasant family. At one end of the tiny house was a stable where the family kept the cow and donkey and a few sheep during the night; in the

LUKE 2:4-7

stable was a manger, with hay for the animals to eat. During their stay, Mary's time arrived and she gave birth to a son. They named him Jesus, and Mary wrapped Him in soft cloths and laid Him in the manger, upon clean hay. It made a perfect little bed for a newborn.

Not far away, shepherds on the hills watched over their flocks during the

LUKE 2:8-12

night. An angel from the Mighty One appeared to them, and the glory of the Mighty One shone all around them, and they shook with fear. The angel said, "Fear not! I bring you good news of great joy for all people! Today in the city of King David, your Savior is born! He is the Anointed One, Sovereign over all! Go now to Bethlehem and find Him; He is lying in a manger."

Suddenly a **MULTITUDE OF ANGELS** appeared in the sky, praising the Mighty One and saying,

LUKE 2:13-14

> *Glory to God in the highest,*
>
> *and on **EARTH** peace and goodwill*
>
> *to men and women whom He favors!*

The shepherds ran through the streets of Bethlehem until they found Jesus, and they told everyone they met what the angels had said.

Now, you're not going to believe this, but you must—because it's **TRUE:** At the *same time* that those jubilant shepherds were running all over Bethlehem, wise astrologers (probably kings), in a **LAND** far, far to the *east* of the Land of Promise, saw a strange star. A really, really **HUGE STAR.** A star no one had ever seen before.

MATTHEW 2:1-12

These wise men studied stars, looking for meanings in them, trying to predict future events. But this star was completely new, having never before appeared in the sky. It moved—westward—and they followed it. For *two years* they journeyed! They said, "This star announces a new king born in Judea, the land of Judah—for that is where it is leading us—to Judea! Let us find the new king, bring him gifts, and pay him homage." The miraculous star led them to Bethlehem, until it stood over the house where Mary and Joseph and Jesus were living. Bowing before the child, the wise men presented Him with gifts fit for a king.

You'll recall, I'm sure, that when Adam and Eve left the Garden of Delights, they went *east*. These wise kings are from the *East*, the place where **SOIL-CREATURES MULTIPLIED** after listening to the awful Serpent. Don't you *see*? It's not just the *Jews* who have a new king, *the whole world does*! When these wise astrologers from the *East* come to find Jesus, it's as if all the nations of the world are coming to find Him! And isn't it marvelous that the Mighty One SPOKE to them in the one language they could understand? The language of the STARS! Oh, I am so excited, I can hardly BREATHE.

DEATHBREATH LURKS IN THE PALACE

Herod the Great, king over the Land of Promise, heard about Jesus, heard about the miraculous star in the sky announcing that a KING was born in Bethlehem of Judea, and he was furious. "No king is going to replace ME!" he bellowed. So he ordered his officials: "Slaughter all the boys in Bethlehem, age two and under!" (The horror!) It was *exactly* what Egypt's Pharaoh had done in Moses' day, killing all Israelite boys under two years old! Warned by an angel in a dream, Joseph saddled his donkey, took Jesus and Mary, and fled with them to Egypt. And that is where they lived until Herod died.

Once again an angel visited Joseph and said, "Herod is dead. Now bring Mary and the child back to the Land of Promise." So they left Egypt in safety, just as the TWELVE TRIBES had left Egypt so many centuries before, and they traveled back to the LAND, the LAND the Mighty One had given to Abraham and his DESCENDANTS.

Do you see what's happening? Well, do you? Even as a baby, Jesus—a DESCENDANT of Abraham *and* King David—is re-enacting the history and journeys of his ancestors! Like Moses, a king wants to kill Him; like the TWELVE TRIBES, He leaves the LAND of Promise, fleeing to Egypt, and there He dwells for years; like them, too, He journeys back to the LAND of Promise, because the Mighty One leads Him out of Egypt and back home. We must watch His every move and listen to His every WORD, or we will never uncover the secrets of the *Ancient Manual*.

CHAPTER TWO

WILD MAN

From THE BOOKS BY MATTHEW, MARK, LUKE, *and* JOHN

MATTHEW,
MARK, LUKE,
AND JOHN

THERE'S SOMETHING I DID NOT TELL YOU. About six months *before* Jesus was born, Mary's cousin Elizabeth and Elizabeth's husband, Zechariah, had a baby boy. He, too, was a miracle baby. You see, Elizabeth and Zechariah were in the same predicament as Abraham and Sarah two thousand years earlier: they were childless. And now, at their age, a baby was impossible. And yet, the Mighty One gave them a son, just as He gave Abraham and Sarah a son!

An angel appeared to Zechariah and said, "Name your son John. He will prepare the people's hearts to meet the Messiah."

John grew into a strong man, but . . . he was odd. He wore clothes made from camel's hair and tied a leather belt around his waist; he ate locusts and wild honey and lived mostly in the desert regions of Judea. He was a wild man. Guess what! The *prophet Isaiah*, centuries earlier, spoke of *John* when he said:

There will be a voice crying in the wilderness:

"In the desert places prepare a way for the great I AM;

ISAIAH 40:3-5   *in the wilderness, make a straight road for God . . .*

And the glory of I AM *will be openly revealed,*

and all the soil-creatures on Earth will see it.

The voice of the great I AM *has spoken."*

The voice crying in the wilderness is . . . Jesus' cousin John!

Throngs of people went into the desert to hear him preach. "Get ready!" he said. "The kingdom of God is coming to EARTH! Repent of your sins! Turn back to the Mighty One!"

They repented—thousands of them—and John baptized them in the waters of the Jordan River. He lowered each one into the muddy waters; and when they came up and out of the water, they felt clean on the inside, cleansed of the sin festering in their hearts.

Question: What on EARTH is "repentance"?

Answer: Why, it means to TURN IN THE OPPOSITE DIRECTION. By *repenting*, the people *turned away from* the dragons and the SERPENT's lies, turning their hearts *toward* the Mighty One, who made them and loves them still. In this way, they prepared themselves for God's GOOD kingdom to arrive, for the Messiah to appear; He would rescue them from their Roman oppressors—or so they thought.

One day while John the Baptist was baptizing, his cousin Jesus approached (He was all grown up now, about 30 years old), and John cried out, "Look! The Lamb of the Mighty One, who takes away the sins of the world!" (Do not forget—I repeat: **DO NOT FORGET**—what the name Jesus *means*! If you've forgotten, go back to Epeisódion II, chapter 1, to find out.) John baptized Jesus, and when Jesus came up and out of the water, John saw the Spirit of the Mighty One, like a dove, descend and rest on Jesus. And John **HEARD** the **VOICE** of the Mighty One declare: "This is my beloved Son, whom I love."

MATTHEW 3:13-17;
MARK 1:9-11;
LUKE 3:21-22

Oh my goodness, I'm getting goosebumps! John the Baptist declared that Jesus is the *Lamb of the Mighty One*. What can that mean? It means that Jesus is a lamb of sacrifice, like the ram that replaced Isaac on the mountaintop. It also means that Jesus is like the Passover lambs whose blood the Israelites painted on their doorposts the night they left Egypt. When the Mighty One saw the blood on the doorposts, He ordered the death angel to *pass over* those houses, leaving their people untouched by Deathbreath.

JOHN 1:29-31

141

Amazingly, John the Baptist announces that **JESUS** is the Passover Lamb— *The* Lamb!

Are you wondering how Jesus can be a lamb? Trust me, it will come clear in a later chapter. For now, think it through a bit: If Jesus is the Passover Lamb, it means He will free Abraham's **DESCENDANTS** from death, just as the ram died in place of Isaac, and just as the Passover lambs in Egypt died in place of Isaac's **DESCENDANTS**.

If Jesus the Lamb can deliver the *Jews* from death, perhaps He can also deliver the *whole world* from death.

CHAPTER THREE

WAR IN THE WILDERNESS

From THE BOOKS BY MATTHEW *and* LUKE

MATTHEW
AND LUKE

AS YOU KNOW, we **SOIL-CREATURES** live now in the Land of Dragons. Ever since the **SERPENT** deceived Adam and Eve with its deplorable lies, it—along with Deathbreath and legions of lesser dragons—rules our globe. Do you not believe me? Well, can you get through even *one day* at school without someone doing something hurtful to someone else? Can you listen to the television news for even *one night* without witnessing the work of dragons? No, you cannot. What, then, are we to do about these horrendous circumstances? We must unlock the secrets of the *Ancient Manual*, that's what we must do! In the *Manual* we learn that the Mighty One has a Grand Plan to *rescue* our world from dragons, to set it (and *us*) **FREE**. I hope you've been noticing how the Plan is unfolding, and I hope you recall my saying a bit earlier that to end the evil in our realm the Serpent and Deathbreath must be *fought*! Those monstrous "its" must be *fought* and **DEFEATED.**

THREE

———

WAR
IN THE
WILDERNESS

1 JOHN 3:8

143

Who *can* and *will* do such a thing?

Allow me to clue you in. One of the later writers in the *Ancient Manual* said this: "Jesus came to **EARTH** to destroy the works of the **EVIL SEA SERPENT**." Do you know what that means?! It means that Jesus will *fight* and *defeat* those two wicked fiends—both the Serpent and its vile companion Deathbreath! Watch what happens.

Immediately after his baptism, Jesus ventured, all alone, deep into the Judean wilderness. It was the Spirit of the Mighty One who led Him there, because Jesus needed to face an ancient foe—the Mighty One's ancient foe, our ancient foe. It was none other than the revolting **SEA SERPENT**, that slithering, lying, boasting, cold-blooded, death-loving viper, that dragon-of-dragons, that **FATHER OF LIES**, the **CHIEF DRAGON RIDER!** This is the enemy that first lied to Adam and Eve; it is the usurper (a pretender, claiming the rights to someone else's throne) that seized control of **EARTH**, the Liar King ruling from its tyrannical and unlawful throne, deceiving and imprisoning everyone in its false kingdom!

Question: What **CURSE** did the Mighty One pronounce on the **SERPENT**?

Answer: "**CURSED** are you! You shall crawl everywhere on your belly and you shall eat dust!"

Question: What **WARNING** did the Mighty One give that newly legless leviathan (monstrous sea dragon)?

Answer: "One day—**ONE DAY!**—a **DESCENDANT** of **EVE** will rise to fight you! You will wound His heel, but do not gloat; for He will **CRUSH** your head!"

At last, the special **DESCENDANT** has arrived. It is Mary's son, Jesus, now fully grown and beginning His mission to **DESTROY THE WORKS OF THE LIAR KING!** Soon He will meet this pretender to the throne; He must go to war against **IT**; and He must win.

Before I tell you about the battle, however, I must tell you more about the special **DESCENDANT** of **EVE**. Yes, yes, we know He will **CRUSH** the Serpent's vile head, but what more do we know about Him? We know much. Because the prophets, sent by the Mighty One during the *Agreement Antīquātus*, gave details. They said:

1. He will be a **DESCENDANT** of Abraham, Isaac, and Jacob/Israel. Well, if He's a **DESCENDANT** of Jacob, then He must be a **DESCENDANT** of one of Jacob's *TWELVE* sons, one of the **TWELVE TRIBES OF ISRAEL**. But which one? Can you guess?

2. Okay, okay, I'll tell you—I've been dying to tell you for ages. It's Jacob's son *Judah*. The **DESCENDANTS** of *Judah* are the people called *the Jews*; therefore the special **DESCENDANT** of **EVE** will be a *Jew*.

3. What's more, the special **DESCENDANT** will be from the lineage of King David, who also came from (you guessed it) the tribe of *Judah*.

4. Not only that, the **DESCENDANT** will be born in David's hometown, *Bethlehem*.

I don't know about you, but I, **SIR WYVERN PUGILIST**, think it is utterly amazing that the special <u>DESCENDANT</u> of <u>EVE</u> (who has come to **CRUSH THE SERPENT'S HEAD**) and the new "King David" (who will free His people from their oppressors and establish a kingdom of perfect justice and peace) are **ONE AND THE SAME PERSON: JESUS!**

THE SPECIAL DESCENDANT OF EVE (WOW!) BEGINS HIS MISSION!

So, as I was saying, Jesus went all alone into the wilderness, where He fasted (didn't eat) for **FORTY** days and **FORTY** nights. **FORTY!** Is that not *exactly* the number of days Noah was in the Ark, through which the Mighty One rescued him from the death-floods? Yes! And is that not *exactly* the number of years the **TWELVE TRIBES** wandered in the wilderness after the Mighty One rescued them from Egypt? Yes!

Do you see what it all means? It means that Jesus is like Noah; He's *the beginning* of a *New* Creation, a *New* Earth. And it means He's like His own people, the **DESCENDANTS** of Abraham, delivered from their bondage in Egypt and heading toward a *new* <u>LAND</u>.

And that is *exactly* why Jesus has gone into the wilderness, because there can be no hope of a *New* <u>EARTH</u>, a *New* <u>GARDEN OF DELIGHTS</u>, until someone faces the **LIAR KING** head-on and **CRUSHES ITS REPUGNANT HEAD!** That battle is between Jesus and the <u>SERPENT</u>; the battleground is the Judean wilderness. Watch what happens.

After **FORTY** *days* of fasting and praying, depending completely on the power of the Mighty One rather than on the power of food, Jesus was exceedingly hungry. That's when the old <u>SERPENT</u> found Him and said, "If you really are the Son of the Mighty One, command these desert stones to become bread." (Remember: Jesus is *starving* for bread.) But Jesus said to that brazen IT, "It is written in the *Ancient Manual*, 'SOIL-CREATURES do not live by bread alone, but by every WORD that comes from the mouth of the Mighty One.'"

MATTHEW 4:3–4;
LUKE 4:3–4

The Serpent tried again. It took Jesus to Jerusalem, up to the Mighty One's glorious Temple, right up to the highest point. Then the devious IT said, "If you truly are the Son of the Mighty One, prove it: Throw yourself off this precipice, for it is written in the *Ancient Manual*:

> *The Mighty One will command His angels to watch over you,*
>
> *And they will hold you up in their arms,*
>
> *So that you cannot strike your foot against a stone.*

MATTHEW 4:5–7;
LUKE 4:9–12

But Jesus answered, "It is also written in the *Ancient Manual*, 'Do not test the Mighty One, who is your God.'" (I believe the Serpent knew FULL WELL that Jesus was the Mighty One Himself, come to Earth wearing human flesh. And yet that arrogant Serpent dared to *test* the God of All. I shudder!)

MATTHEW 4:8–11;
LUKE 4:5–8

The shameless Serpent, now dripping with contempt, took Jesus to a high mountaintop and showed Him all the powerful and magnificent kingdoms of the world. "All of these I will give to you," the Serpent grinned venomously, "if only you will bow down and worship ME."

Jesus commanded the old Sea Monster, "Away from me, you Father of Lies! It is written in the *Ancient Manual*, 'Worship the Mighty One, whose name is *I AM*, the One True God; serve only Him!'"

Then the Serpent, utterly defeated, left Jesus, and (as the words of the *Ancient Manual* do indeed declare) angels from the Mighty One surrounded Him and held Him up in their arms.

That is the great war Jesus fought in the wilderness against our ancient foe. What—did you expect swords and shields? Well, **DID YOU!** Oh, my friends, no dragons are ever slain with such weak weapons; no mere sword can inflict a death-blow to the Serpent! The greatest weapon of the Mighty One is **TRUTH. TRUTH, TRUTH, TRUTH!** It strips the lying reptiles of all their powers and shrivels them into nothings.

The Serpent will return, though, wounded and weakened. For this is not the last battle.

CHAPTER FOUR

THE NEW TWELVE

From THE BOOKS BY MATTHEW, MARK, *and* LUKE

MATTHEW, MARK,
AND LUKE

AFTER JESUS' WAR AGAINST THE SERPENT in the Judean wilderness, He traveled north to the region of Galilee. His mother, Mary, was from Nazareth in Galilee, and that is where Jesus grew up. He knew this place well.

One day, as He walked beside the sparkling Sea of Galilee, He saw two brothers, Simon Peter and Andrew. They were fishermen and were casting

MATTHEW 4:18-20;
MARK 1:16-18;
LUKE 5:1-11

their nets into the **SEA**. Jesus called to them, "Come and follow me, and I will make you fish for men and women!" Simon Peter and Andrew dropped their nets, jumped out of their boat, and followed Jesus.

A bit farther up the shore, Jesus spied two other brothers, James and John (nicknamed the Sons of Thunder), who also fished. There they were, just sitting in a boat mending their nets, when Jesus called to them: "Come and follow me!" And they, too, left their nets and their boat—and their father and their employees—and followed Him.

MATTHEW 4:21-22;
MARK 1:19-20;
LUKE 5:1-11

All in all, Jesus called **TWELVE** men to be His close disciples. **TWELVE!** What does it remind you of? Why, of course: the **TWELVE TRIBES OF ISRAEL!**

Everyone **DESCENDED** from any one of the **TWELVE** tribes of Israel knew that it was through *them*, their people, Abraham's **DESCENDANTS**, that the Mighty One would send a great deliverer to save them from their enemies. They also knew that it was through *them*, their people, that the Mighty One would **BLESS** all the nations of **EARTH**. They didn't really know how that would happen, but they believed it was true.

And now you can see why the number **TWELVE** is so important. It points to the **TWELVE TRIBES OF ISRAEL**, Abraham's children. The Mighty One promised that *they* would bring His **LIGHT** to the world, and His great **BLESSINGS**. But how?

First, they would tell the rest of the world about the Mighty One, whose personal name is *I AM*. As the **SOIL-CREATURES** of the world watched the lives of the **TWELVE TRIBES**, the other nations would see that the Mighty One was *with* the **TWELVE TRIBES**, and *helped* them, and *provided* for them. Second, through the **TWELVE TRIBES**, the Mighty One gave the Ten Laws, to point **SOIL-CREATURES** to Himself, and to teach them what love looks like. Third, it would be through *them*, the **TWELVE TRIBES**, that the special **DESCENDANT** of **EVE** would arrive to **CRUSH** the **SERPENT'S** head, freeing the entire **EARTH** from that usurping tyrant-dictator and its unscrupulous torturer, Deathbreath.

If through the **TWELVE TRIBES** the Mighty One wants to **BLESS** and free the **ENTIRE EARTH**, will He not **BLESS** and free *you*? Are you not one of His beloved **SOIL-CREATIONS**, made in His own **IMAGE**? Dear reader, you are! He loves you beyond imagining.

You can see, then, how very important it was for Jesus to choose **TWELVE DISCIPLES**. It was Jesus' way of announcing to the world: "I am the special **DESCENDANT** who has come from **EVE**, and from the **TWELVE TRIBES**—to set the world free!"

Now, you won't believe this because it's so amazing, but you must, because it's **TRUE** (and I already hinted at it in the previous chapter): Sometime later, Jesus announced to His **TWELVE** that not only was He their promised Messiah, *and* the new "King David," *and* the special descendant of Eve, He was the great *I AM* himself! Yes, you read that correctly: **JESUS IS THE GREAT *I AM*.** He is the Mighty One who revealed His name to Moses at the burning bush! He is the One whose Presence dwelled in the Tabernacle and the Temple! Do you see what's happened? The Mighty One has come to our world wearing **SOIL-CREATURE FLESH**, as a **MAN**, so that we can see Him, and talk with Him, and know Him once again, just as Adam and Eve once did. Remember how He came to Mount Horeb in the wilderness, and there was fire and smoke and the mountain quaked? He kept moving closer and closer to the **TWELVE TRIBES** until He began living in a tent in the *very center* of their camp. Now He has come *even closer than that*, for now He is clothed in a soil-creature body, walking and talking among us! Is it not too astounding to believe?! Yes, except that it's true. *Oh, Truth!*

ANNOUNCEMENT: There is yet another name for Jesus. Perhaps you've guessed it—if you read my book ***Dragon Slayers***, you know it already. Allow me to introduce you to . . . the **CHIEF DRAGON SLAYER** (blessed be His name forever!)

CHAPTER FIVE

THE CHIEF DRAGON SLAYER AND THE AGREEMENT NOVUS UN=PARALLELUS

From THE BOOKS BY MATTHEW, MARK, LUKE, *and* JOHN

MATTHEW, MARK, LUKE, AND JOHN

T HE CHIEF DRAGON SLAYER and **THE TWELVE**, and many of His close women followers too, traveled together all over the Land of Promise. He announced to his people—the Jews—that the Kingdom of God had arrived and they should trust Him and follow Him.

SECRETS
of the
ANCIENT
MANUAL
REVEALED!

152

Everywhere He went people flocked to hear Him teach. He healed the sick, the paralyzed, and the lepers with dreadful skin diseases. From Galilee in the north to Jerusalem in the south, He longed to repair his broken, suffering Creation.

Some people recognized who He was—the Mighty One, the Creator—and they worshiped Him. Others despised Him, for they believed He was nothing more than a man who had no business claiming to be God. But what no one could yet see was that Jesus was about to establish a *New Agreement* (in other words, a new *Covenant*): *the Agreement Novus Un-Parallelus.*

Let me explain. Remember when the Mighty One rescued the Israelites from Egypt and gave them the Ten Good Laws? Of course you do. Well, forgive me, but I didn't tell you everything.

What's that I hear? You're saying, "Why not?" Well, perhaps I didn't want to, that's why! It's very difficult, trying to convey so much information. And now I am quite exhausted from all this writing, writing, writing . . . why, I've hardly slept a wink since beginning chapter 1, and now my fingers are about to **FALL OFF!** And I'm **CRACKING UP FROM STRESS!**

(Oh dear, oh dear, please forgive the outburst—it was the dreadful dragon Frantix attacking me. How I despise that colossal dragon-of-busyness! It strikes every time a deadline approaches.)

Now, here's the part I didn't tell you. After the Mighty One rescued Abraham's descendants from Egypt, He gave them Ten Laws, gave them to Moses on Mount Horeb, and He made a **COVENANT** (a forever agreement) with them: They promised to keep the Ten Laws and He promised to give them land and protect them and never ever leave them. (Yes, yes, **I KNOW** you already know that part. **PULEEZE** quit tormenting me, and keep reading!)

Here's the part you *don't* know: Ancient covenants were sealed in *blood*—the blood of a slain animal. (It was all very gory, but that's what life was like in the ancient world.) The people on each side of the agreement declared that if they ever broke their side of the covenant, they would become like the slain animal: Dead. Covenants were serious.

That is how things worked under the *Agreement Antīquãtus*: the Israelites promised to keep the Mighty One's Good Laws, and the Mighty One promised to give them land and never leave them.

But you'll also recall (oh, I *do* hope you were paying attention!) that the people **FAILED MISERABLY** at keeping the Law! They lied, cheated, and murdered; they worshiped the false gods of the Canaanites and forgot all about the great *I AM* who had delivered them from Egypt. They *broke* their side of the covenant, and to break a covenant meant *death*.

But let me ask you this: Do you **REALLY BELIEVE** that *any* of Abraham's descendants (or any other soil-creature for that matter) could completely keep all those Good Laws? C'mon, do you? It was **HOPELESS**, I tell you, **HOPELESS!** And the Mighty One *knew* it was hopeless. They couldn't keep those Laws anymore than we can. Long, long ago we were infected by the Serpent's lies, and we agreed to follow its creepy ways; it commandeered Earth's throne and it rules over our world with a scepter of *injustice*; and if you don't believe such a thing, might I ask you to spend one day reading the headlines of news around the world? Do you live in a just world ruled by love? No, you do not. If you think you do, then you are **GREATLY DECEIVED.**

So of course **NO ONE** could keep the Law, not completely! But *knowing* and *loving* the Ten Laws was (and **IS**) so very important. The Law shows us **WHO THE MIGHTY ONE IS.** He loves life; He does not lie, or cheat, or steal; He does

FIVE

THE CHIEF
DRAGON
SLAYER AND
THE
AGREEMENT
NOVUS
UN-PARALLELUS

153

not murder; and He is the One True God of All, glorious in beauty and perfect love. How He longs for His creatures to love each other as He loves them! So even though no one could fully keep the Law, just *wanting to keep it* is what mattered. A person who *loved* the Law was a person who *loved* the Mighty One, *trusted* Him, and *believed* His Words. The Law *pointed* soil-creatures to the Mighty One. But the Law—in and of itself—could *save* no one. Because it could not defeat the Serpent! Well then, are we without rescue?!

Question: What does the name Jesus mean?

SECRETS
of the
ANCIENT
MANUAL
REVEALED!

154

Answer: It means "*I AM* saves."

If the Laws cannot save, but *I AM* can and does save—and Jesus *is I AM*— then it is *Jesus* who saves!

Now here's where it gets even more **AMAZING.**

Question: Who is the one true Passover Lamb?

Answer: It is Jesus.

Question: How were ancient covenants sealed?

Answer: With the blood of a slain animal.

ANNOUNCEMENT: Jesus will become the "slain animal" whose blood will seal a **NEW COVENANT**—not a covenant for the **DESCENDANTS** of Abraham only, but a covenant between the Mighty One and *all* **SOIL-CREATURES**. In this **NEW COVENANT**, the Mighty One, through Jesus, promises to destroy the **SERPENT** and Deathbreath and to share with us *His own* **LIFE** and **BREATH**, the only **LIFE** and **BREATH** that *can* keep the Law, that *can* love and do what is **GOOD**. In this

NEW COVENANT the Mighty One also promises to *re-create the world*, to make a *New* **GARDEN OF DELIGHTS**, and to *re-make each of us*, freed from the powers of **EVIL** and death. All of those promises stand on His side of the **NEW COVENANT**. What then is on *our* side of this new agreement? What must *we* promise to do? All we do is *trust* Jesus, the Great Deliverer, the Mighty One wearing soil-creature flesh. He gives us everything we need, and we simply *trust Him.*

FIVE

———

THE CHIEF
DRAGON
SLAYER AND
THE
AGREEMENT
NOVUS
UN-PARALLELUS

155

Question: Where is the blood to seal the **NEW COVENANT**?

Answer: It is in Jesus! He is the Lamb of the Mighty One! His own blood will seal the New Covenant.

And that is how things work under the *Agreement Novus Un-Parallelus*. Jesus makes a forever agreement (the *New Covenant*) between Himself (He is the Creator) and the entire Creation, and He seals it himself. All the promises made are on His side of the agreement. Our part is to come to Him in *faith:* simply *trust* Jesus, the Chief Dragon Slayer, to do it.

REALLY BIG SURPRISE: This is, in fact, how things actually worked under the old *Agreement Antīquátus*, too. It's just that no one could see it back then. Abraham became the Mighty One's **F-R-I-E-N-D** because he *trusted* the Mighty One. And Abraham's descendants, who lived under the Ten Laws, even though they could not consistently *keep* all of the Law, *trusted* that the Mighty One would **ONE DAY** send a deliverer to free them from their dragonish ways and the oppression of the tyrant dragon-of-dragons that had set itself upon Earth's throne.

So, you see, the Mighty One's Grand Plan to rescue His **EARTH** and His beautiful **SOIL-CREATURES** from the **SERPENT** and Deathbreath has always worked by . . . *faith*.

(But we're getting ahead of the story.)

SECRETS
of the
ANCIENT
MANUAL
REVEALED!

156

CHAPTER SIX

THE TAMING OF THE SEA

From THE BOOKS BY MATTHEW, MARK, *and* JOHN

MATTHEW, MARK, AND JOHN

JESUS TALKED TO HIS PEOPLE about the Ten Good Laws. Many (not all) of the Jews thought they were *so good* at keeping the Law that they did not need a deliverer! (PULEEZE! Did they think they were PERFECT?) Apparently, the religious leaders believed they were and even said so publicly. Have you met the type? If not, I suggest you listen to ME when I'm under Braggen's attacks. Oh, the self-righteous things I say when I allow that dragon to torment me! Hideously embarrassing! Braggen has been around since the Serpent crawled out of the Sea, so it's not surprising that the religious leaders of Jesus' day believed they needed **NO ONE** to rescue them from evil and death. It was, of course, just a big **LIE** they had swallowed whole. I suppose at their funerals the wailers wailed, "But why did he **DIE?** He was so **GOOD!**"

SECRETS
of the
ANCIENT
MANUAL
REVEALED!

158

MATTHEW
22:36-40;
MARK 12:28-31;
LUKE 10:25-28

So Jesus tried to explain to them that the Law, in itself, could never make them righteous, as the Mighty One is righteous. It could only *point* them to Him. Jesus said to them, "If you are so good at keeping the Law, then why do you ignore the poor and the sick? Why are you so greedy? Why do you lie and cheat?"

He tried to tell them to think about the Law in a new way—that the *entire thing* could be summed up in two simple statements: (1) Love the Mighty One with all your being; and (2) Love your neighbor as you love yourself. (Well then, let me just ask you this: If a person claimed to be oh-so-good at keeping the Law but he or she did **NOT** love his or her neighbors, then **HOW COULD HE OR SHE BE KEEPING THE LAW?** And if he or she did **NOT** love his or her neighbors, then **HOW COULD HE OR SHE TRULY LOVE THE MIGHTY ONE?**)

They needed help. Try as they might, not one of them could perfectly keep the Law. That's why they needed the Great Deliverer, and so do we (I repeat: **SO DO WE!**).

There are many, many stories I could tell you about the Chief Dragon Slayer when He walked the paths of Earth, but alas, I have not enough space. I promised to reveal the *secrets* of the *Ancient Manual*, showing the bright threads that run straight through it, so I shall limit myself to a few key events—such as this one:

It was time for the spring Passover Feast, but Jesus and **THE TWELVE** had *not* gone to Jerusalem for the celebration. Instead, they spent the day on the far side of the sparkling Sea of Galilee. Twenty thousand peasants followed them there, to see Jesus perform miracles. Most had walked all day to see Him, and most were poor, with little food. They were hungry. Jesus told them to sit down on the grass. **THE TWELVE** found a young boy carrying five small loaves of bread and two tiny fish, but what was that among twenty thousand? Holding the boy's humble meal, Jesus gave thanks for it, broke it into pieces, and fed **ALL TWENTY THOUSAND PEOPLE** from that little bit of food! The bread just kept **MULTIPLYING**! It was like the manna sent to the Israelites in the wilderness every morning for **FORTY** years! It just kept coming!

MATTHEW 14:13-21; MARK 6:32-44; LUKE 9:10-17; JOHN 6:1-13

Jesus then said to the crowds—oh, it's so amazing I can barely speak it—He said: "*I AM* the bread of **LIFE**." **WOW!** Jesus called Himself "*I AM.*" It's the Mighty One's personal name, the name He revealed to Moses at the burning bush! Jesus tells twenty thousand people that *He* is the great *I AM.* Why I—

JOHN 6:30-35

YIKES! I just fell off my chair!

Okay, back at the keyboard. There's more: Jesus also said He is the **TRUE BREAD** upon which we must feed, for (as it says in the *Ancient Manual*) "soil-creatures cannot live on **EARTHLY** bread alone, but by every **WORD** of the Mighty One." These are the very words He quoted to the **SERPENT** in the War in the Wilderness, when that lying brute tempted Him to turn stones into bread. Don't you see? Jesus is our true "manna" in the wilderness, our true "bread," the very **WORD** of the **MIGHTY ONE**, the **WORD** that **SPOKE** everything into existence *in the beginning*, the **WORD** that sustains every *BREATH* of *LIFE*—

YIKES! Fell off my chair again!

Well, after Jesus fed that entire multitude, evening approached and He slipped away secretly. **THE TWELVE** had no idea where He was, so they jumped into a boat and began rowing back across the Sea of Galilee to the town of Capernaum.

DARKNESS fell. When they had gone exactly halfway, a howling wind stirred up the waves and wrapped its arms about their boat, tossing it to and fro upon the now violent SEA. It was a monster storm.

Winds shrieked and battered the boat, while the men labored hard at the oars.

In the DARKNESS, the figure of a man loomed—walking upon the waves!—approaching them! "Look!" they screamed. "It's a spirit! We're doomed!"

Jesus called to them, "It is I! Do not be afraid!" That is what the "spirit" said, and it was so much like the words the Mighty One SPOKE to Moses in the burning bush: "*I AM.*" It was their Lord's voice. But how could *He* be walking to them upon that untamed SEA? No one can walk upon the SEA—no one but the Mighty One Himself. (Exactly!) Every good Jew knew that. Why, it's stated in the *Ancient Manual*, in several places! And yet there was Jesus—walking upon the SEA! THE TWELVE trembled. "Get in our boat, get in our boat!" they begged Him. He did, and *immediately* they reached the shore of Capernaum! No need to row any further; they were delivered, right then and there, from the chaotic terrifying waves, for the Mighty One SPOKE to the SEA and calmed it, and He deposited THE TWELVE safe and sound on the GOOD LAND He had created.

CHAPTER SEVEN

THE LAST LAMB

From THE BOOKS BY MATTHEW, MARK, LUKE, *and* JOHN

WARNING: A lot of bright threads will soon come together. The meanings of many *key words* will soon be revealed. Keep tracking them, and **STAY AWAKE!**

MATTHEW, MARK, LUKE, AND JOHN

A T LEAST **SEVEN TIMES** Jesus called Himself "*I AM*"—by which He was saying that He and the Mighty One are *the same.* And by saying it **SEVEN** *times* (reminding us of the **SEVEN** days of Creation), He was saying that *He*, Jesus of Nazareth, was, and *is*, the Creator. The Jewish religious leaders were **OUTRAGED!**

162

Jesus got into even more trouble: During a visit to Jerusalem, He entered the Mighty One's glorious Temple and proclaimed: "I will tear this Temple down and in *THREE DAYS* I will rebuild it!" (THREE DAYS!)

At first the authorities mocked Him, saying, "Ha! It's taken 46 years to build this Temple, and you think you're going to rebuild it in *three days*?" But what Jesus meant is that *He* was now the Temple—His *own body* was now the place where the Mighty One dwelled on EARTH. If his *body* was destroyed, He would raise it back to life in *three days*.

The Jewish leaders were furious. "Anyone claiming to be God is a blasphemer," they roared, "and must be executed!" But He slipped away from their sight.

Spring arrived again, and this year Jesus and THE TWELVE traveled to Jerusalem to celebrate the joyous Passover Feast. Like all the other pilgrims choking the streets and inns of the city, Jesus and THE TWELVE would eat a meal of roast lamb and unleavened bread to commemorate the wondrous night when the Mighty One led their ancestors out of Egypt.

On the day they slaughtered the Passover lambs, each family took its slain lamb and slowly roasted it over hot coals. As the day wore on, the mouthwatering smells of roasting meat wafted into every nook and cranny of Jerusalem. Soon the feasting would begin.

Jesus and THE TWELVE gathered in an upper room, secretly, because the

Temple police had determined to arrest Him. At their Passover party, Jesus gave THE TWELVE a NEW LAW—just like the Ten Laws given to Moses, but this one is even greater: LOVE ONE ANOTHER. In a sense, it wasn't a new law at all, because the Mighty One had already given a similar Law to Moses, saying,

"Love your neighbor as you love yourself." But this "new" Law was special, because it was to be the **ONE LAW** governing all of Jesus' followers, all the citizens of the new kingdom of peace that He will one day establish on Earth. It is the Law of Love: **LOVE ONE ANOTHER**. Here's what's so amazing about it: In His one Law, Jesus summed up the entire Ten Laws! Do you know what that means? It means that if you keep the Law of Love, you will, in fact, be keeping *all* the Good Laws—for in loving your neighbor, you will be loving the Mighty One who created your neighbor. It's simply impossible to love your neighbor and not love your neighbor's Maker!

LOVE ONE ANOTHER: It's what the Ten Good Laws had been saying all along.

Then He invited **THE TWELVE** to sit down for their Passover meal. He took a loaf of unleavened bread, gave thanks for it, broke it into pieces, and gave it to them, saying, "Take and eat. This is my *body, offered* for you." Wide-eyed, each disciple took a piece of bread and ate it. But His words—what could they mean? The only *bodies offered* for the Feast were those of the Passover lambs. How could *Jesus* be their lamb? Well, let me ask you this: Do you remember the words that John the Baptist proclaimed about Jesus? You do **NOT**?! Dragon Slayer, have you been **SLEEPING?! WAKE UP, WAKE UP!** Okay, I'll tell you, but only because I'm trying to practice Jesus' *new Law:* **LOVE ONE ANOTHER.** When he saw Jesus walking toward him, John the Baptist shouted: "Behold the Lamb of God, who takes away the sins of the world!" Do you also recall my telling you that Jesus is the *one true* Passover Lamb? You do? Oh, good. (More on this below.)

Later in the meal, Jesus picked up a cup of wine. He gave thanks for it and then said to **THE TWELVE**, "Drink this, all of you. It is the **NEW COVE-NANT** in *my blood, shed* for *you*." (*The Agreement Novus Un-parallelus!*)

MATTHEW 26:26;
LUKE 22:19

MATTHEW
26:27-28;
LUKE 22:20

Oh, my goodness! John the Baptist's words are true after all! Jesus *must* be the Passover Lamb, because it was the *shed blood* of the lambs that saved the Israelites from death. Dragon Slayers, do you see what this means? It means that the Passover lambs offered so long ago on that night in Egypt, the night of the Exodus, were not the *true* ones; they only *pointed* to the true one. There is only *one* Passover Lamb, and now He sits at dinner with THE TWELVE. All the previous lambs, offered through the centuries to commemorate the Exodus, merely *foreshadowed* the real one. What's more, the ram caught in the thicket on the mountain where Abraham planned to sacrifice Isaac—that ram *also foreshadowed* the One True Lamb. In fact, ALL sacrificed animals under the *Agreement Antīquátus* were merely signs of the *actual* Lamb of God who ALONE can deliver the Israelites, AND THE WORLD, from Deathbreath!

Each disciple took a drink from the cup of wine, until it had gone all 'round the table, trying to understand what exactly the NEW COVENANT was.

MATTHEW
26:21-25;
MARK 14:17-21;
LUKE 22:21-23;
JOHN 13:21-30

Then Jesus said, "One of you is about to betray me."

"No!" they protested. "We would never betray you, Lord!" Some asked, "Who is it, Lord? It's not me, is it?"

He answered, "It is the one who dips his bread in the bowl with mine." To their horror, it happened: One of them dipped his bread in the dish at the same time Jesus did. It was Judas Iscariot. Immediately, Judas fled the feast.

MATTHEW
26:26-46;
MARK 14:32-42;
LUKE 22:40-46

After supper, Jesus asked His remaining ELEVEN disciples to walk with Him to a GARDEN, a place called Gethsemane—a garden very *unlike* the GARDEN OF DELIGHTS. Into that DARK and dreadful night they walked. When they came to Gethsemane He stopped and asked the men to remain there while He went farther, alone. "Stay awake!" He warned them. "Keep watch for me! And pray!"

Going some distance, He threw himself on the ground and cried, "O Father-God, if it's possible, take away this awful cup that I must drink! Nevertheless," He wept, "not my will but yours be done."

Going back to **THE ELEVEN**, He found them fast asleep. "Could you not watch with me for one hour?" He asked. "Watch! And Pray! So that you will not be tempted!"

Is it not one of the easiest and most beguiling temptations of all—the temptation to simply **FALL ASLEEP?** Have you ever done it in school? Perhaps in church? Maybe during a movie? Ach! I fall asleep all the time. Why, even while working on this important little book, I have fallen asleep. **AND SO HAVE YOU!** I caught you snoozing at the beginning of this chapter! Allow me to impart some wisdom for you to carry through life: When it comes to following Jesus, you must *stay awake*. By that I mean *stay awake* to the dangers surrounding you in this Land of Dragons, lest you fall victim to those reptiles' deceptive wiles. (As the disciples have now done in Gethsemane.)

Aha! If they're in danger of *temptation*, as Jesus says they are, then the *tempter* must be near; and who is the *tempter* if not the old **SEA SERPENT**! The ancient foe that sorely tempted Jesus in the wilderness, that sorely tempted Adam and Eve in the **GARDEN OF DELIGHTS**, was undulating in the **DARKNESS**, silently slithering into the **GARDEN** of Gethsemane.

THE GREAT AND
FINAL BATTLE

MATTHEW, MARK,
LUKE, AND JOHN

I JOHN 3:8

IN THE GARDEN OF GETHSEMANE, Jesus knew His hour had arrived—His hour to offer Himself as the Passover Lamb and to complete His mission to **DESTROY THE WORKS OF THE SERPENT**. Now the **GREAT BATTLE** was upon Him. No one could fight it for Him, or with Him. He alone must face the cold vile Serpent.

Question: How long will the awful battle persist?

Answer: Will it be *forty days and nights*? No. *Seven days*? No. You see, a span of *forty days and nights* is a sign that the Mighty

One's Grand Plan of rescue is moving forward. And a span of *seven days* always whispers, *Creation, Creation, Creation,* reminding us that the Mighty One will *remake* His Creation! But this battle will last neither *forty days* nor *seven days*. Well then, how many? I'm not telling you—yet.

EIGHT

THE GREAT
AND
FINAL
BATTLE

167

Let me explain. The **GREAT BATTLE** Jesus now enters is neither a *forty-day* fight nor a *seven-day* one, because *before* the Mighty One can either *rescue* or *remake* the Creation, He must utterly defeat both the Liar King *and* its henchman-torturer, Deathbreath (yes, the battle will mean *death*). Did you get that? Before the Grand Plan of rescue can move forward, and before the Earth can be re-created, the Serpent and Deathbreath must be conquered.

And that is why the **GREAT BATTLE** will persist for exactly (I've been dying to tell you this for ages) **THREE DAYS**. It will be like the plague of darkness in Egypt, darkness as dark as the grave, lasting *three days*.

Think about it: It took **THREE DAYS** for Abraham and Isaac to journey to the mountain of sacrifice. During those **THREE DAYS**, Isaac was as good as **DEAD**, because Abraham intended to sacrifice him on the mountaintop. But when Abraham raised the knife to slay his son, the Mighty One **STOPPED** him, saying, **"DO NOT HARM THE BOY!"** That is the moment when the Mighty One provided a ram to sacrifice in place of Isaac. At the end of those **THREE** agonizing **DAYS**, Isaac—dead man walking—is "raised" to new life; his "resurrection" *foreshadows* Jesus' own defeat of Deathbreath, soon to be accomplished in a span of **THREE** agonizing **DAYS**.

THE GREAT BATTLE BEGINS

SECRETS
of the
ANCIENT
MANUAL
REVEALED!

168

JOHN 18:4-6

Back in the Garden of Gethsemane, after Jesus finished praying, He returned to His disciples and once again found them **ASLEEP**! Do you see what I mean? It's such a beguiling, innocent-looking temptation, but at the wrong time it can be devastating! Jesus nudged His slumbering disciples. "Get up now," He said. "The hour has arrived. My betrayer is here."

There were shouts, the loud clanking of swords and staves, torches lighting up the night. Judas Iscariot emerged from the **DARKNESS** at the head of a band of soldiers and priests from the Temple. (The priests had promised to pay Judas thirty pieces of silver if he handed Jesus over to them.) Jesus said to them, "Whom do you seek?" They said, "Jesus of Nazareth." And He answered, "*I AM* He." At the sound of the Mighty One's sacred name, they fell to the ground.

Once more He asked them, "Whom do you seek?" They trembled: "We seek Jesus of Nazareth." And He said to them again, "*I AM* He."

Then Simon Peter, one of **THE ELEVEN**, drew his sword and struck the high priest's servant, slicing the young man's ear right off his head. Jesus commanded Peter, "Put your sword away! Do you think I should not drink the cup of suffering my Father-God has appointed me to drink?" Then He healed the man's severed ear, as if Peter had never struck it at all.

They bound Jesus and took Him to the house of the high priest to be tried. The high priest and all his council gathered together and questioned Him. Many so-called witnesses spoke up, telling lies about Jesus. The council looked hard for false evidence to use against Him, evidence to take to the Roman authorities to convince them to execute Jesus. But they could find no evidence at all—**NONE!** Finally, two witnesses testified against Him, saying, "This rabble-rouser said, 'I will destroy the Temple and raise it back up in **THREE DAYS**.'" (Reader, now you know why Jesus made this strange statement about the Temple. He was announcing what was going to happen: He was saying that He will offer His body—which is now the Mighty One's Temple—to Deathbreath but will defeat the life-killing monster in the space of **THREE DAYS**.)

Hearing those words, the high priest stood up and said to Jesus, "What have you to say to that charge?!"

Jesus said nothing.

The high priest hissed, "I demand you tell me, under oath: Are you the Messiah, the Son of God?"

Jesus said, "Yes, it is true. In the future, you will see me sitting at the Mighty One's right hand and coming on the clouds in glory."

In a rage, the high priest ripped his own clothes. "He speaks blasphemy! Why call any more witnesses? Council, what is your verdict?!"

"He deserves death!" they clamored. They spit in His face, and they punched Him with clenched fists.

Then the Temple guards took Jesus to the Roman governor of their province, whose name was Pilate. "Are you the king of the Jews?" Pilate asked Him.

MATTHEW
27:11-26;
MARK 15:2-15;
LUKE 23:1-3
AND 13-25;
JOHN 18:28-40;
JOHN 19:1-16

"Yes," said Jesus. "What you say is true." The Jewish priests and leaders, who had accompanied Jesus to see Pilate, then shouted all sorts of accusations against Him.

Jesus said nothing.

Mystified, Pilate said to Him, "Do you not hear their accusations; do you not have anything to say to them?!"

Jesus said nothing.

He wondered at Jesus' silence, thinking, *Why doesn't he try to defend himself?*

Pilate said to the crowds, "It has been my practice, during your annual Passover Feast, to release for you whatever prisoner you choose. I have in my prison a notorious criminal: Barabbas. Should I release Barabbas or Jesus?"

They shouted as with one voice: "Barabbas! Give us Barabbas!"

"Barabbas? What then should I do with Jesus your Messiah?"

"Crucify him!"

"Why? What has he done? I can't find one crime he's committed!"

"Crucify him!" they roared even louder. "Cru-ci-fy him!"

Pilate got nowhere reasoning with the crowds, so he gave up. He took a basin of water and washed his hands in front of them. "You see this," he blurted. "My hands are clean in this matter. If you want to crucify Jesus, crucify him. But I'll not bear the guilt of it, not me!"

Soldiers forced Jesus to carry the hideous wooden cross on His back. Oh, my! He's like Isaac! Isaac, who carried the wood for the burnt offering (the offering of himself) on *His* back (see p. 60). They drove Jesus, stumbling and broken, to the crucifixion-hill, the place where soldiers fastened criminals to wooden beams and left them to writhe in anguish for days, until they died.

Savage Roman troops nailed Jesus to a cross and hoisted it upright against the vast blue sky overlooking Jerusalem. They sat down to watch. Hours passed, terrifying hours: The **SUN** went **DARK**; **EARTH** shook; stones rolled away from tombs and God-lovers from the days of the *Agreement Antīquátus* walked out of their graves! Onlookers believed a cosmic battle waged somewhere beyond their vision. It did! Even as He hung on the hideous torture-cross, Jesus fought His ancient foe, the **SERPENT**. Not with

SECRETS
of the
ANCIENT
MANUAL
REVEALED!

170

MATTHEW
27:32-44;
MARK 15:21-32;
LUKE 23:26-43;
JOHN 19:17-24

MATTHEW
27:51-53

human weapons, not with human power, but with the powers of **TRUTH** and **LOVE**—the truth about **EVIL** and the self-sacrificing love of the Mighty One for His **CREATURES**. Oh, my dear reader, words can never express the depths of the Mighty One's love for you—you who are His own beloved **SOIL-CREATURE**.

We don't know what all happened, because the battle was not visible to **SOIL-CREATURE** eyes. But I believe the **SERPENT** pierced Jesus the God-man with lie after lie after lie, tempting Him to worship the **SERPENT** (the horror!), promising Him rescue. It coiled its twisting length 'round the splintered beams, unhooked its viperous jaws, dripped deadly venom from its pointed fangs; it hissed and spit and lashed with stupendous force its vehement tail, shrieking and yowling, letting loose its most sinister powers to undo life; but God-in-Flesh absorbed the brutal assaults into Himself until the **SERPENT** had fully exhausted its hideous black wrath. Then Deathbreath lunged, chomping at its bit, and the writhing **SERPENT** unleashed its depraved pet. The cosmic struggle raged as Deathbreath did its worst . . . then choked . . . and spit . . . groveled in distress . . . for Jesus **SPOKE**; and His words rang out across the entire **EARTH**: **"IT IS FINISHED!"** Then He bowed His head and He *gave up* his spirit.

Oh, Dragon Slayers, do you realize what happened? Deathbreath did *not* kill Jesus! Jesus *gave up His own life*! No one could take it from Him, no one! He is the very source of **LIFE** and **BREATH**, so only He possessed the authority to lay it down. And that is what He did, for He is the one true sacrifice, the Passover Lamb who is pure self-giving love.

EIGHT

THE GREAT
AND
FINAL
BATTLE

171

JOHN 19:28-30

MORNING HAS BROKEN!

From THE BOOKS BY MATTHEW, MARK, LUKE, *and* JOHN

MATTHEW, MARK,
LUKE, AND JOHN

IT ALL HAPPENED ON A FRIDAY—the crucifixion, that is—the sixth day of the week, and the seventh day, the Sabbath, approached, for evening fell suddenly upon them; so His friends took Jesus' body down from the cross and buried Him quickly in a borrowed tomb, finishing just before the *day of rest* officially began—at sundown on Friday. (A new day began *not* at sunrise, but at sundown the previous day.) So you see, the burial happened so quickly, the women had no time to anoint Jesus' body with extra spices.

They waited *three days* (*three days!*). Then, very early, well before dawn, Mary of Magdala and some of the other women who followed Jesus crept silently through the darkness, to His tomb. Sickened by Friday's gruesome events, they dreaded encountering the ruthless soldiers. **CAN YOU BELIEVE THESE FEARLESS WOMEN, NOW SNEAKING THROUGH THE DARKNESS?!** They witnessed the entire crucifixion, yes they did! Even as the **ELEVEN** disciples fled in terror (except for John, a Son of Thunder), these brave women remained, unmovable to the bitter end. I cannot imagine what they saw: Roman malevolence (viciousness) defies description! It turned the stomachs of its observers inside out; it bestowed upon its witnesses a permanent inner shudder, a profound horror to forever scar their minds and hearts. Why, I shudder even to think of it!

And yet these women—these **AMAZING** women—ventured through that most dangerous darkness to visit Jesus' tomb! Oh, these were true Dragon Slayers, I tell you, true Dragon Slayers! In all my days of slaying evil reptiles, never (despite my renowned courage) have I possessed *their* courage—never, ever!

Well, it was now the first day of the week, Sunday, and (as I said) the *third day* (according to the strange method of counting days back then) from Jesus' crucifixion: Friday itself, Day One; Saturday (the Sabbath), Day Two; now Sunday, *Day Three.*

OH MY GOODNESS, I FORGOT TO TELL YOU, I PLUM FORGOT: He died far sooner than expected, far earlier than death normally comes from crucifixion. I hate to inform you, I really do, but death by crucifixion takes *days.* Jesus died within *hours.* Some thought they heard Him say, "Father, into your hands I commend my spirit." Why, He appeared to have power over His own death,

LUKE 23:44-46

as if He had given up His life at the time He *chose*, rather than waiting for death to steal Him. Well, of course He did! Have I not already said—probably a million times—that He is the *very source* of LIFE? If He is LIFE itself, how then could anyone—or any *thing*—take LIFE from Him? Impossible! Jesus was not a helpless victim—no, no! He *offered* Himself to Deathbreath, willingly. Why? So that He could DEFEAT that cold-blooded, life-despising "it," that's why.

Now I must get back to telling you about these AMAZING WOMEN.

MATTHEW 28:1–10;
MARK 16:1–8;
LUKE 24:1–9;
JOHN 20:1–10
In the DARKNESS (Shhh! . . . read this part *quietly*) Mary Magdala and her friends approached the tomb—but slowly—uttering not a word, creeping ever closer, like stealthy, silent lions, so as not to alert the Roman guards who were surely keeping watch.

Suddenly, the EARTH jolted, wobbling and pitching like untamed waves. Just like at Mount Horeb, when God arrived . . . *after three days* (see p.80)!

The tombstone! It rolled from the entrance and a man dressed in white, shining from head to toe as bright as a lightning bolt, sat upon it! BRIGHT LIGHT EVERYWHERE! So exceedingly bright, Roman guards lay on the ground like dead men! The angel spoke (he SPOKE!) to the women, "Fear not! You come looking for the body of Jesus, who was crucified. But He is not here. He is risen from the dead! See, the tomb is empty! Go back into Jerusalem and tell the disciples He is going ahead of you to the region of Galilee. That is where you will see Him for yourselves. I was sent to tell you this."

Fast as shooting stars, the women ran back into the city to find THE ELEVEN.

JOHN 20:11–18
But Mary of Magdala left them, running back to that empty grave, and there she stood, alone, outside the tomb, in a GARDEN. Oh . . . my . . . goodness . . . she's in a GARDEN (and I think she's about to walk and talk with the great *I AM*)! Unconsoled by the bright angel's words, she wept and wept because

Jesus' body was gone. *Gone!* Who could have taken it? Who would commit such a treachery? If only she knew where the thieves had laid the body, she would find it and anoint it.

JOHN 20:12-18

A man walking in the **GARDEN** said to her, "Woman, why do you weep in such sorrow? Whom do you seek?"

He must be the gardener, she thought. She answered, "They've taken away my Lord, and I don't know where they've laid him."

The man said, "Mary." When she heard Him say her name, exactly as He had always said it, she knew who it was: Jesus! Just as the angel had declared: Jesus lived! Risen from death!

She clutched Him and cried, "My teacher, my teacher!"

"Run!" He commanded her. "Run and tell the Eleven that I am risen!!"

Mary ran back into Jerusalem, and when she found **THE ELEVEN**, she said breathlessly, "I've seen Him . . . with my own eyes . . . I've seen the risen Lord!"

Are you thinking what I'm thinking?

Question: Who was the first person to believe the **SERPENT'S** lies?

Answer: Yes, you're right—it was Eve, a woman.

Question: Who is the first person to see the risen Jesus, the One who defeated both the Serpent and Deathbreath?

Answer: Yes, you're right—Mary of Magdala, a woman. Isn't that grand? Only the Mighty One could do something so marvelous and compassionate.

Do you not think that Eve suffered awfully, knowing that *she* was the first to have eaten the deadly fruit from the Tree of the Knowledge of Good and Evil? Do you not think that all other FEMALE SOIL-CREATURES have also suffered because of her decision? They have. For since time immemorial there have always lived MALE SOIL-CREATURES (some, not all) who have loved to abuse them, treating them no better than animals in a pen, using Eve's beautiful name (Mother of All Living) as a derogatory (insulting) accusation against FEMALE SOIL-CREATURES made in the Mighty One's own IMAGE: "Eve ate the fruit first," they snarl, "and you are nothing more than she, nothing more than Eve; we despise you!" I can tell you that the Mighty One ABHORS such words and deeds! They come directly from the stinking, loathsome SERPENT, from its deepest pit in the Sea of Chaos. How I detest that abusive monster!

Do you see what Jesus is doing? By choosing Mary as the *first soil-creature* to witness Jesus' resurrection, He says to his entire Creation, "Whereas EVE was the first to shut her eyes against me, inviting Deathbreath into the world, now this 'Eve' is the first to see me risen, victorious over Deathbreath forever!" In Jesus, EVE is transformed, made *new!* Jesus, who is *merciful and gracious, slow to anger and abounding in lovingkindness*, delivers Woman from *shame* and crowns her with the greatest *honor*.

Dragon Slayers, we cannot help but follow Him!

Question: On what day of the week did Jesus burst forth from His tomb?

Answer: On the morning of the *first* day—Day One of the new week.

SECRETS
of the
ANCIENT
MANUAL
REVEALED!

176

EXODUS 34:6

Oh, I can hear what you're saying! You're saying, **"I GET IT, I GET IT, SIR WYVERN PUGILIST! LET ME TELL IT, LET ME TELL IT!"** Well, go ahead then: **TELL IT!** (Trust me, I can hear you! You're shouting my ears off!)

"The day of Jesus' resurrection from death is Day One of the **NEW CREATION!** It reminds us of Day One of the original Creation, when the Mighty One said, 'Let there be **LIGHT**!'"

Yes, yes, yes, Dragon Slayer—you are absolutely **CORRECT!**

Question: If the day of Jesus' resurrection is Day One of the *New* Creation, then who is the first soil-creature of the *New* Creation?

Answer: Why, it's the risen Jesus, of course! He is the new "Adam" in a whole new Creation! And everyone and anyone who hangs on to Him will **ALSO** become a *wholly new* **SOIL-CREATURE!** (I'm absolutely **SERIOUS!** I'm not making this up—it is stated in the *Ancient Manual* for all to read!)

I can hear what you're saying: "But Sir Wyvern, **I DON'T GET IT!"** **PULEEZE, WOULD YOU STOP SHOUTING! YOU'RE HURTING MY EARS!**

Let me explain, let me explain. As the Passover Lamb, Jesus gave up His own **LIFE**, for *us*, to save us from Deathbreath. Indeed, He passed *through* death. What I mean to say is that He truly did *die*, He was **IN THE GRAVE**; but Deathbreath could not *hold* Him there! After *THREE DAYS*, Jesus conquered Deathbreath, bursting forth from the tomb, never to die again. Never, ever! Deathbreath can do *nothing* to Him, and I mean *nada, nothing*! And so you see, if we hang on to *Him*, He will bring *us* through death as well, and we will come out on the other side of it, **ALIVE! RESURRECTED!**

Is it not too **GLORIOUS** to grasp? The risen Jesus is *the beginning* (think of the first chapter of Genesis) of the **NEW CREATION!**

Oh yes, Dragon Slayer, morning has broken indeed!

CHAPTER TEN

THE GREAT UNSEEN

From THE BOOK CALLED ACTS

ACTS

FTER JESUS ROSE FROM HIS GRAVE, He was different. That is to say, His *body* was different. It was transformed in so many ways, no longer subject to the limitations of bodies living on an **EARTH** controlled by the tyrannical **SERPENT**. Oh, there was no doubt that Jesus' resurrection body was a true **SOIL-CREATURE** body, no doubt at all—it had flesh and bones! And still does! Jesus is *forever* resurrected! (Did you get that? Jesus is in His resurrection body *forever*.) But the **LIFE** of His new body is not dependent on blood, not at all. Its **LIFE** is the **LIFE** of the Creator, the great *I AM*. Jesus' new body comes *not* from the realm of **EARTH**, but from the

SECRETS
of the
ANCIENT
MANUAL
REVEALED!

180

realm of the Mysterious Three (wait for chapter 11). As such, it was sometimes fully visible to **THE ELEVEN**, and to the women disciples who followed Jesus. Other times, Jesus' body was *not* visible to Earthly eyes in this Earthly realm.

Nevertheless, Jesus appeared—visibly—in His amazing God's-realm body to His disciples over and over again, for *FORTY* days. Now, I can read your mind, Dragon Slayer. You're remembering: After the *FORTY*-*day* flood, God began the Creation all over again, with a cleansed **EARTH**, and He told Noah's family to be *FRUITFUL AND MULTIPLY* and **FILL** the **EARTH** once more.

Why, you've been paying attention! Hooray! Anything else you'd care to share? What's that? I can hear you, go on: "After the Israelites wandered for *FORTY* years in the wilderness, having escaped slavery in Egypt, the Mighty One brought them into a New **LAND**, *foreshadowing* a whole new world; and after Jesus fought the **SERPENT** for *FORTY* days in the desert, He later entered a great cosmic battle against the **SERPENT**, even passed through *death*, but after *THREE DAYS* He conquered Deathbreath, to begin a **NEW SERPENT-FREE, DEATH-FREE CREATION**."

Yes, yes, Dragon Slayer, you're absolutely right, and I must praise you for your profound insights! I can see where you're going with this. You're saying that, when Jesus appeared to His followers for *FORTY* days after His resurrection, it was His way of saying, "I'm *beginning* a new world—just as I did after the flood, just as I did in bringing the Israelites to the **LAND** of Promise. Only *this* New Creation is the *real one*—the one the others only *foreshadowed*." Yes! Yes, yes, yes, you've got it right!

During those incredibly joyous *FORTY* days after His resurrection, Jesus ate meals with His friends, and He discussed the *Ancient Manual* with them, showing them all the passages that pointed to *Him*, that showed *He* was the DESCENDANT of EVE (oh, such an honor for Eve!) who would one day—ONE DAY!—arrive to CRUSH the SERPENT'S head. And now He has, He has!

MATTHEW 28:18-20

At the end of the *FORTY* days, He told THE ELEVEN, and his other followers, too, to go into all the world and declare the good news to all SOIL-CREATURES: **THE DESCENDANT OF EVE HAS ARRIVED AND HAS FREED THE WORLD FROM ITS BONDAGE TO THE SEA SERPENT AND DEATHBREATH!**

"Now I will go away and you will not see me for a while," Jesus told His followers. "But wait in Jerusalem until the Comforter, my own Spirit, comes upon you. I am sending Him to you soon and I will be with you always."

ACTS 1:4-5

Jesus climbed a mountain and THE ELEVEN gathered 'round to watch what He would do. As they watched, He *vanished from their sight*! They looked up to the clouds, hoping to see Him, and just then two men appeared and said, "Why do you look for Him? This same Jesus, whom you just saw disappear, will one day return to your sight in the same way you saw Him go."

ACTS 1:9-11

Greatly puzzled, THE ELEVEN returned to Jerusalem—and waited.

While they waited, the Feast of Pentecost arrived, the annual spring harvest festival fifty days after Passover. Suddenly, there was a great BREATH of wind from heaven, rushing with a deafening roar through the house where they sat waiting. Tongues of fire danced on their heads, yet they were not burned, just as tongues of flame had danced in the burning bush that Moses saw, yet the bush was not burned up.

Reader, by now you've probably come to understand that when the One True God of the Universe, the Mighty One whose name is *I AM*, *appears* on Earth, or *speaks aloud* to His soil-creatures, there is often fire—not destructive fire, but holy fire. Mountains quake and smoke; sometimes trumpets blare. I know you have observed these phenomena as you've read this, my little book. Which is why *I* know that *you* know that these mysterious tongues of fire dancing on the heads of Jesus' followers are, in fact, the Presence of the Mighty One, the Presence of Jesus Himself! Yes, it is the arrival of the Comforter, the name Jesus gave to His own Holy Spirit. The Comforter filled Jesus' followers—FILLED THEM!

What can it possibly mean to be FILLED with the Comforter? I DON'T KNOW—not completely. But I know some things about it, because I've experienced it myself, as has every Dragon Slayer, whether he or she truly knows it or understands it. Think of it this way: You are not merely a body, are you? Heavens, no! You also possess a mind or intellect—and a soul or *spirit*. Your *spirit* is the part of you that is unseen but is the essence of who you are. Not that you were meant to live *only* as a spirit. No, no! The Mighty One created you to be both *spirit* and *body*, and one day Jesus will give you a *new body*, like His glorious new body. But getting back to your *spirit*—I think you know full well that there is a big part of *you* that is unseen, that is *spiritual*. The Mighty One is also a S*pirit*—although He took on a body in Jesus. Nevertheless, He is still a *Spirit*. When Jesus returned to the Mighty One's realm, unseen by us now, He sent his own Spirit—which is also the Mighty One's own Spirit—to live within us. When the Spirit of Jesus fills us, He fills our own spirits, communing with us in that part of us, comforting us, dwelling with us, deep within our beings, *walking and talking with us*. It's a mystery, I know, but it's true. (*Oh, Truth!*)

Now you understand why I call the Comforter the *Great Unseen*. Though you cannot see Him, He is very, very real. As I said, He is the Spirit of the Chief Dragon Slayer, and the Slayer sends Him into our hearts to dwell *with* us! Now the Mighty One has moved as close as He possibly can to his soil-Creatures, as close as close can be.

The disciples, going outside to meet the crowds after the Spirit-Comforter had filled them, began speaking . . . well, you're not going to believe this but I swear it's true! . . . they began speaking in *other languages* (YES, OTHER LANGUAGES, LANGUAGES THEY HAD NEVER SPOKEN BEFORE!) as the Comforter enabled them.

Because it was the Feast of Pentecost, Jews from every nation of the world had come to Jerusalem. They heard THE ELEVEN speaking in other languages, and each person in the crowd heard the words in his or her *own* language! They said to each other, "Are these men not Galileans? How is it that we hear them speaking in our own languages?"

WOW! Do you remember the Tower of Baby Talk? Well, do you? At that tower the Mighty One—way back in prehistory—divided the nations, separating their languages so they could not so easily work together to spread the Serpent's dragonish ways. But Jesus has now DEFEATED the Serpent, so the Comforter is now REUNITING THE NATIONS! Why, they can understand each other! Think of the words they're hearing, words explaining to them that Jesus is the DESCENDANT of EVE, the Mighty-One-in-Flesh, who came and CRUSHED the Serpent's head!

Peter and the rest of THE ELEVEN stood before the crowd, and Peter called out, "Listen, all of you! What you see happening today is what the prophet Joel, whose words are recorded in the *Ancient Manual*, said would happen:

> *The Mighty One says, 'In the last days*
> *I will pour out my Spirit on all soil-creatures . . .*
> *On both men and women, I will pour out my Spirit . . .*
> *And every person who calls on the name of the great* I AM *will be*
> *saved.'*

ACTS 2:14-24

Peter continued: "People of Israel, listen! Jesus of Nazareth performed miracles and signs among you to show you He was from the Mighty One. You know this is true! Wicked men put Him to death on a cross; but the Mighty One raised Him from death, freed Him from its sufferings because Death-breath possessed no power to hold Him.

ACTS 2:36

"My fellow Israelites, I tell you the truth: Jesus of Nazareth, whom your religious leaders crucified, is the Messiah—and Lord of All!"

CHAPTER ELEVEN

THE MYSTERIOUS THREE

From throughout THE ANCIENT MANUAL

THROUGHOUT THE
ANCIENT MANUAL

I T WASN'T UNTIL AFTER JESUS' "ASCENSION" (the event *FORTY days* after His resurrection, when He disappeared from Earthly view, returning to the Mighty One's realm) that His followers started to put it all together, the mystery of the Mighty One: the fact that the Mighty One is actually *Three*, yet definitely only *One*.

Jesus, when He was still with **THE TWELVE**, had spoken of the mystery, saying, "I and the Father are One." And, "I will send my Spirit, the Comforter, to you." But they had not understood.

JOHN 10:30;
JOHN 14:16-18

Even the *Ancient Manual*, under the *Agreement Antīquátus*, had hinted at it, but no one grasped it.

To this day no one fully understands it. Of course, just because a person cannot understand something doesn't mean it's not true. Things that are true are true whether you understand them or not. Your understanding something doesn't *make* it true, nor does your *not* understanding it make it *not* true. (Do not forget this.)

But as I was saying, it wasn't until after Jesus' ascension that His followers began putting it together—this mystery of the Mighty One. You see, the Mighty One is One-in-Three and Three-in-One. It sounds unbelievable, I know, but that's the only way I can say it; however, it does **NOT** mean that the Mighty One is three separate Gods—no, no, no! The Mighty One is **ONE GOD**, the One-and-Only God. But within the Mighty One, is (or should I say "are"?) three persons. Three persons who are so close to each other and who love each other so much, each constantly looks outward to the other two, so they are really **ONE** person, only **ONE**—and yet, the **ONE** is **THREE**.

Now, I know what you're thinking. How can one person be three persons, and how can three persons be one person? **I DON'T KNOW!** I am only a humble Slayer of dragons, as are you (I hope). All I am saying is that the Mysterious Three is something I cannot fully explain. No one can. And I might point out that if we *could* understand these difficult mysteries, we would not call them *mysteries*. We would call them *clarities*, or something like that.

Suffice it to say that, after Jesus' ascension back to His Father-God, His early followers realized that this is one truth He had been trying to teach them all along: That He, the Son of God, is One with the Father-God, because God is One-in-Three and Three-in-One. We even have names

SECRETS
of the
ANCIENT
MANUAL
REVEALED!

186

for each of the Three-in-One: There is the **PATER PERFECTUS** (the Perfect Father, or God the Father), the **CHIEF DRAGON SLAYER** (who is the Son of God, Jesus), and the **COMFORTING GHOST** (who is also called the Holy Spirit). Together, they are the Mysterious Three, the Mighty One, whose personal name is *I AM*.

(You've probably noticed that, when referring to Jesus, I have been using "Him" or "He," with a capital H—just as I call the Mighty One "Him" or "He," with a capital H; for Jesus, as you can now see, is truly God-in-Flesh.)

CHAPTER TWELVE

A NEW GARDEN OF DELIGHTS

From THE BOOK CALLED REVELATION

REVELATION

I HEAR **EXACTLY** WHAT YOU'RE SAYING, yes I do! You're saying, "Why, if Jesus defeated the **SERPENT** and Deathbreath, are those two fiends still around? And why do **SOIL-CREATURES** continue to follow the **SERPENT'S** lies, committing all sorts of **EVILS**? And why does Deathbreath still extinguish LIFE?" (**NOTE:** I am underlining, and you should be too. Just because we're nearing the end of this little book does **NOT** mean you should slack off on your **ASSIGNMENT!**)

Well now, those are excellent questions and I'm glad you asked them.

The answers begin with this crucial reminder: **DO NOT FORGET WHAT YOU LEARNED IN CHAPTER 10:** Jesus will return! He will, He truly will! He told His disciples He would go away for "a while." And at His ascension, when He vanished from view, two mysterious men (angels?) appeared and said, "This same Jesus, whom you just saw disappear from your sight, will one day *return* to your sight in the same way you saw Him go."

KNOW THIS FACT: When Jesus returns to Earth, He will *finish* the work He began when He was here the first time.

Let me explain. The first time He was here, He utterly defeated Deathbreath. That monster could not hold Jesus in the grave, because nothing can snuff out the life of the **GOD OF LIFE.** Nevertheless, Deathbreath still roams our world, attacking every living thing, cutting off its breath. But Deathbreath's time is very, very, very limited. Its powers are now *weak* and *temporary*. It may *appear* to you that Deathbreath is the most powerful force imaginable, but it is **NOT!** The Mighty One is infinitely more powerful than the wizened (shriveled up) Deathbreath. For a short time, Deathbreath is permitted to thrash its hideous tail against all and sundry. But what you *cannot see* with your Earthly eyes is that, when Deathbreath administers *death*, it no longer has the power to actually *kill*—at least not permanently, not without the Mighty One's approval. You see, if you simply hang on to Jesus, the Chief Dragon Slayer, you cannot die! Oh, you will pass through the *process* of death, but just like He did, you'll come out on the other side of it, to new and forever **LIFE.** By hanging on to Jesus, *you* get to share in the new life of *His* resurrection!

Ach! I forgot to tell you one of the most important things Jesus ever said. He said, "The person who believes in me, even if that person dies, will live;

and the person who lives, because that person believes in me, will **NEVER DIE**." Wow!

NOTE: Over two thousand years ago, when He walked our Earth, Jesus *conquered* Deathbreath. But when Jesus *returns* to Earth, He will *destroy* Deathbreath forever. Death itself will die! (I repeat: **DEATH WILL DIE!**)

At this point, we cannot understand why the Mighty One delays in sending the Chief Dragon Slayer to finally and totally destroy Deathbreath, but it has something to do with waiting for more and more soil-creatures who side with evil to forsake their dragonish ways and turn to the Mighty One for life. The Mighty One is extraordinarily patient and is not willing that any soil-creature should perish by siding with the Serpent. He longs for *every* soil-creature to trust Him and know Him, to walk and talk with Him, and to enjoy His abundant and good blessings.

When it comes to the Sea Serpent, the same things are true as with Deathbreath. In the War in the Wilderness, Jesus wielded the weapon of **TRUTH**, striking down the viper's twisted, odious lies. Nailed to the cross, Jesus exhausted the leviathan's furious vengeance against the Mighty One, absorbed into Himself its dark and hideous strength, inhaled the rotting vile stench of the old Sea; until writhing in defeat, the snake fell to the dust in a withered coil. From that moment, it began the countdown to its own demise. It is still here, but now it slithers across our globe on borrowed time. Sure, it continues to dispense lies all over our world. And sure, it recruits many, many followers to perform untold evils in its service. It loves to gloat, telling its followers (I will not mention names) that it wins most of its battles against the Mighty One; but that is only a pitiful lie. It will continue to wreak havoc on Earth, but only for a time. It lives in quaking fear of the Chief Dragon Slayer's

SECRETS
of the
ANCIENT
MANUAL
REVEALED!

190

return to Earth, when He will *bind* it—that horrendous dragon-of-dragons, that loathsome Chief Dragon Rider, that Liar King—with unbreakable chains and cast it into the depths of the Sea of Chaos—**FOREVER.** Never again will it get loose. Earth will be freed and Deathbreath will be no more!

On that glorious day, the Chief Dragon Slayer will set up His good and righteous and perfect kingdom on Earth. He will unveil the *New Earth*, the *New Garden of Delights*, free of lies, disease, fear, hatred, oppression, injustice, poverty—and murder. Abel, whose blood has been crying out from the ground since the beginning of time, will be **RESURRECTED!** *All* who love the Mighty One will be resurrected, just as Jesus was resurrected! And their new bodies of flesh and bone will be like His glorious body.

ISAIAH 51:3
EZEKIEL 36:35-36
REVELATION 21:1-2

ZECHARIAH
2:10-11;
REVELATION 21:3

Then the dwelling of the Mighty One will be with His soil-creatures, and He will wipe away all tears from their eyes. Death will be no more. The Sea will be no more. The curse on the ground will be no more. The waters of life will flow from the throne of the Mighty One and of the Lamb of God. On *either side* of that rushing river will stand the Tree of Life, with the waters of life coursing straight through its base! Do you remember the **TREE OF LIFE?** It was in the original Garden of Delights, not far from the Tree of the Knowledge of Good and Evil. When Adam and Eve left the Garden, the Mighty One put angels and a flaming sword to guard the entrance, so that Adam and Eve could not *return* to the Garden and *eat* from the Tree of Life and live forever in their fallen condition.

ISAIAH 25:8
REVELATION 7:17

ISAIAH 25:7-8A
REVELATION 21:1, 4

REVELATION 22:3

REVELATION 22:1-2

GENESIS 3:22-24

But when the New Earth is revealed (the *New* Creation begun by Jesus' resurrection), they *can* and *will* return—to the *New* Garden of Delights—because the Serpent will be forever banished, and soil-creatures will be made anew, free of lies and every kind of evil. There the Tree of Life awaits them—it awaits *us*. Every month it bears the most delectable rich fruits; and its leaves (oh, how I love this part), its leaves are for the *healing of all the nations on Earth*. Did not the Mighty One promise that through Abraham's descendants He would bless the entire world? Is not Jesus the special descendant of Eve, *and* Abraham, *and* David? He is, oh indeed He is!

REVELATION 22:5 In the *New* Garden of Delights, there will be no darkness, and no night. No lamps will be needed, not even the lamp of the sun, because the Mighty One is there, the great *I AM*, and Jesus, the Chief Dragon Slayer, who once announced to the crowds: "*I AM THE LIGHT OF THE WORLD. WHOEVER COMES TO ME WILL NEVER WALK IN DARKNESS BUT WILL HAVE THE LIGHT OF LIFE.*"

JOHN 8:12

Try to imagine it: The glorious New World revealed when the Chief Dragon Slayer returns to Earth!

I know, I know—you can hardly wait for it, can you?!

Nor can I.

REVELATION 22:20 "Even so, come, Lord Jesus!"

A MISSIVE FROM
SIR WYVERN PUGILIST

MY DEAR DRAGON SLAYERS (for each of you bears that title, if not yet, then soon),

Thus ends my little book, ***Secrets of the Ancient Manual Revealed!*** There are many, many more stories to tell from the *Ancient Manual*, but, alas, I must save them for another volume.

I hope you followed the crucial *key words*, and I hope you began to spot the bright threads woven through the *Manual's* vast fabric. If you did, you are now another keeper of the great treasures of the *Manual*, many of which have been buried for eons. But you must not *hide* the treasures you've acquired. No, no, no, you must **NOT**! The secrets of the *Ancient Manual* were never *meant* to be secret, but to be **NOISED ABROAD**. It is the dragons and their followers who strive to bury them (and bury them they have, for far too long), so that no one can enter the circle of the *Manual's* **GREAT LIGHT**.

Your task, should you be ready to accept it, is to *tell others the* Manual's *wondrous secrets*. As you know, it is a difficult book, a most difficult book. But you are now trained in its mysteries; and in the areas where you remain a bit confused, you need only go back and re-read my excellent explanations. My book is not intended to be read and then stuck upon a shelf. No, no, no! It is meant to be kept and studied and used often. The more you read it, the deeper will grow your understandings of the mysteries, for they are not simple. But they are true. **OH, TRUTH! OH, TRUTH, FORSAKE US NOT!**

Readers, I shall miss you. But I do hope you will visit my B-L-O-G (such a silly word, I cannot say it), which you can find at **www.dragonslayersbook .com**. When I am not away battling revolting dragons, I will post messages full of news and expert tips on the arts and practices of slaying the wretched beasts that **MAKE ME PUKE!** I will also share more insights on additional secrets hidden in the *Manual*. You can also write to me personally, the old-fashioned way, using pen and paper. Send your letters to: **Sir Wyvern Pugilist, P.O. Box 6972, Minneapolis, MN 55406, USA**. No, I do not live in Minneapolis, but my secretary does.

Now, **PULEEZE** watch out for dragons; and **PULEEZE** keep studying the *Ancient Manual*, for you dare not journey through this Land of Dragons without access to its wisdom. Hang on always to the Chief Dragon Slayer (blessed be His name forever!), who loves you more than words can express and whose Comforting Ghost watches over you as you await the Slayer's return, the unveiling of His kingdom of genuine love and justice, for He hears your cries, He has defeated your ancient foes, and *through Him* you shall be **RESURRECTED!**

I remain your faithful and loyal teacher,

Sir Wyvern Pugilist

Sir Wyvern Pugilist

Slayer of a Thousand and One Dragons (and counting)

SECRETS
of the
ANCIENT
MANUAL
REVEALED!

194

GLOSSARY

Aaron Moses' older brother who helped Moses speak to Egypt's wicked king. Unfortunately, he made the golden calf the Israelites worshiped after escaping slavery in Egypt.

Abel He and Cain were Adam and Eve's first children. Violently killed by his brother Cain, Abel is the first human murder victim.

Abhor To despise, hate, or loathe something or someone (see also *loathe*). *I abhor roast aardvark for dinner.*

Abraham Approximately 4000 years ago he heard the Mighty One call him to leave his city and go to a new land prepared for him and his descendants. He is the ancestor of the ancient Israelites and the Jews of today.

Adam The Mighty One's most glorious creation and the first human, made in the Mighty One's own image.

Ancestor (see also *descendant, offspring*) A person in your family line who lived long before you. *My ancestor Sir Kayoss Pugilist the Firm was my great-great-great-great grandfather.*

Antīquátus Something old, from the past, replaced by something new and better.

Ark A chest or box, small or great, for holding something special. *Noah's ark held all the seeds of the original Creation.*

SECRETS
of the
ANCIENT
MANUAL
REVEALED!

196

Babel, Tower of The exact details are lost in the mists of prehistory, but its purpose was to allow its builders to climb to the so-called gods. It means "Tower of Babbling" because it was there that the Mighty One divided human language.

Beguile To deceive or trick someone. *I am often beguiled by Braggen, who persuades me that boasting makes me extra-special.*

Bless To grant special favor, honor—even glory—to someone or something. *The Mighty One blessed the seventh day, setting it apart as a day of rest.*

Blood The substance that keeps life flowing through an Earthly body. *When the animal's blood was spilled, its life was spilled.*

Burnt offering (see also *sacrifice*) A special animal-sacrifice offered to the Mighty One by ancient Israelites; it was offered whole, showing wholehearted devotion to the One True God.

Cain He and Abel were Adam and Eve's first children. Violently killing his brother Abel, Cain is the first murderer.

Canaan/Canaanites An ancient and warring tribe that lived in the Land of Promise—the land the Mighty One promised to give to Abraham and his descendants.

Chaos (see also *cosmos*) A condition of complete disorder and confusion, referring especially to the ancient formless Sea the Mighty One drove back at the dawn of Creation.

Chief Dragon Slayer (see also *Mysterious Three*) Another name for Jesus. As the Mighty One come to Earth in a human body, He is fully God and fully man. He alone can destroy all the dragons of evil.

Comforting Ghost (see also *Mysterious Three*) Also called the Holy Spirit, the Comforting Ghost is One with the Mighty One and Jesus, encouraging us and teaching us about Jesus' great love for us.

Conceive To become pregnant with a baby; or to think up a new idea. *Their first baby was conceived about the same time they conceived the idea to move to Alaska.*

Cosmos/cosmic (see also *chaos*) It means order (as opposed to disorder and confusion) and is also used as a name for the entire universe as a system of order and harmony. *The Cosmos sings with the music of the spheres.*

Covenant A formal and binding agreement made between two people or groups. In the *Ancient Manual* it is the binding agreement made between the Mighty One and the ancient Israelites: they promised to keep His Good Laws, and He promised to never leave them.

Curse/cursed The opposite of a blessing. Instead of goodness bestowed on a creature or thing, harm will come to it. *The Mighty One cursed the Serpent because it lied to Adam and Eve.*

Deplorable Something so terrible, so bad, it causes regret or grief. *Sir Wyvern made a deplorable decision when he chose to listen to Braggen.*

Descendants (see also *ancestor, offspring*) The people in your family line who come after you and directly from you—your children, grandchildren, great-grandchildren, etc.

Divine Warrior Another name for the Mighty One, especially when He comes with His heavenly angels to fight the Sea Serpent and its evil dragon-servants. Jesus is the Divine Warrior appearing in human flesh to conquer the forces of evil and death.

Eden, Garden of The *Garden of Delights*: the special garden the Mighty One created for Adam and Eve and the other creatures—a place of safety, goodness, and harmony that existed before the Serpent entered.

Egypt The ancient country (see your first map) in which Abraham's descendants, the Israelites, were horribly oppressed and enslaved for 430 years.

Elijah One of the great prophets of the Mighty One who spoke the Mighty One's words to the Israelites. He was taken up to God's realm; he did not die.

Elizabeth The mother of John the Baptist, Jesus' cousin.

Enoch A very ancient man who *did not die* because the Mighty One took him into His (God's) own realm.

Epeisódion A fancy name for an event (an episode), or for a long series of events which, together, make up a long episode of time.

Eve Adam's wife. She is another "Adam," the second of the Mighty One's most glorious creation, made in the Mighty One's own image.

Evil Anything that opposes the Mighty One's goodness and love; any force that destroys life, causing harm and hurt; the drive to do wrong things.

Exodus To go out, to leave a place (think of the word "exit"). When it begins with a capital E, it refers to the night the Israelites left Egypt. *Moses led the Exodus from Egypt.*

Foreshadow To show or imply that something is going to happen in the future. *The early storms foreshadowed a summer of rain.*

Fruitful Full of growth, producing more plants, more fruit, more creatures. *Rabbits are so fruitful, they produce too many bunnies to count.*

Gabriel The Mighty One's great messenger-angel, whose name means "God is my Hero."

Galilee The northern region of the Land of Promise, where Jesus grew up.

Garden of Delights (see *Eden*)

Genealogy A listing or account of a person's ancestors and descendants. *My genealogy reveals generations of courageous Dragon Slayers.*

Genesis It means "beginnings" or "origins," and is the name of the very first book in the *Ancient Manual.*

"gods" Any thing or any one that we bow before and worship in place of the One True God, Maker of Heaven and Earth.

Goliath The giant Philistine warrior who taunted the Israelite army and was slain by David, who used only his sling shot. The word now refers to any problem or force that appears huge and frightening. *Some goliaths of the sports industry believe they can lie about taking illegal drugs.*

Good/goodness Everything that comes from the Mighty One, reflecting the Mighty One's right doing, honesty, justice, wholeness, truth, and love. The very opposite of evil.

Grace Love, favor, and mercy bestowed on us without our earning them. *The Mighty One rescues us from sin and death purely by His acts of grace.*

Hic Svent Dracones "Here are dragons" (in Latin).

Holy "Set apart"—for service to, or worship of, the Mighty One—or the Mighty One Himself, for He is set apart from all other beings in this world. *The* Ancient Manual *is a holy book, revealing the holiness of the Mighty One.*

I AM The Mighty One's personal name, which He told to Moses when He spoke to him from the burning bush.

Idol Any person or thing that is worshiped in place of the One True God. Or, the wood, stone, metal, or plastic object that represents the false god. *The "Almighty Dollar" is nothing more than a modern idol.*

Iniquities Another word for "sins" or "evil doings" or "wicked acts."

Isaac Abraham and Sarah's only son, through whom the Mighty One promised to give Abraham countless descendants.

Israel/Israelites (see also *Jacob*) Another name for Jacob, Abraham's grandson. *The descendants of Israel are the Israelites.*

Jacob (see also *Israel*) Abraham's grandson whose name the Mighty One changed to Israel. From his twelve sons came the Twelve Tribes of Israel.

Jebusites The people of a pagan tribe who inhabited the city of Jerusalem in the Land of Promise. King David drove them out.

Jerusalem The city of the pagan Jebusites, conquered by David, who made it the capital city of the Land of Promise.

Jesus Another name for the Chief Dragon Slayer, who is the Mighty One come to Earth clothed in human flesh, making him fully man and fully God. The name Jesus means "*I AM* saves."

Jews, the Descendants of the tribe of Judah, from the Twelve Tribes of Israel; the name of the modern descendants of the ancient Israelites.

John the Baptist Jesus' cousin who paved the way for the arrival of Jesus the Messiah.

Joseph Jesus' Earthly father.

Joshua Moses' assistant, the great warrior who led the Israelites into the Land of Promise after they had wandered for 40 years in the desert. The name Joshua means "*I AM saves*" (as does the name Jesus).

Land of Nod The "Land of Wandering" to which Cain was banished after he murdered Abel.

Land of Promise The land on the east coast of the Great Sea (the Mediterranean) that the Mighty One promised to Abraham and his descendants.

Loath Very unwilling. *I am loath to go anywhere without the Chief Dragon Slayer*. (Compare to *loathe* and *loathsome*—DO NOT mix them up!)

Loathe To feel total disgust for something. *Oh, how I loathe dragon breath*. (Compare to *loath* and *loathsome*.)

Loathsome Something that causes hate or disgust. *Deathbreath is the most loathsome of all dragons*. (Compare to *loath* and *loathe*.)

Manna The miraculous food the Mighty One sent to the Israelites every morning during their 40 years of wandering in the desert. It means "What is it?"

Mary The girl the Mighty One chose to become the mother of Jesus the Messiah, who is God-in-flesh.

Messiah It means "the anointed one," the one sent by the Mighty One to deliver the Jews from their enemies. It is a title for Jesus.

Midian A pagan country beyond Egypt, where Moses fled when Pharaoh wanted to kill him.

Mighty One The One True God of All, Maker of Heaven and Earth, source of all life.

Miracle An event that simply (according to the laws of Nature) cannot happen in our world, except by an act of the Mighty One.

Mount Horeb The mountain in the Sinai desert where the Mighty One revealed Himself to Moses in a burning bush, and where—years later—He gave him the Ten Good Laws (also called the *Mountain of God* and *Mount Sinai*).

Mount Sinai (see *Mount Horeb*)

Moses When he was a 3-month old baby, his mother hid him in a basket in the River Nile, thus saving him from Pharaoh's death squads; as an older man, he led the enslaved Israelites out of Egypt.

Mysterious Three Another name for the Mighty One, who is One-in-Three and Three-in-One (also called the *Trinity*). The Three are: the Pater Perfectus, the Chief Dragon Slayer, and the Comforting Ghost.

Nazareth A little town in the northern region of the Land of Promise where Jesus grew up.

Nile, River The river running through Egypt, it provided ancient Egypt with water for its vast croplands.

Noah The righteous man through whom the Mighty One saved His Creation during the Great Rescue. Noah built a giant ark; his name means "*rest*."

Nomad A person who lives in tents and moves from place to place.

Novus Something entirely new and amazing (from Latin).

Offering (see *sacrifice*)

Offspring (see also *ancestor, descendants*) A person's child, or all of his or her children.

Pater Perfectus (see also *Mysterious Three*) Also called God the Father, He is One with God the Son (who is Jesus, the Chief Dragon Slayer) and One with the Comforting Ghost.

Pharaoh The title used by the rulers of ancient Egypt.

Philistines A seafaring, warring tribe in the Land of Promise, they lived by the Great Sea and became one of ancient Israel's chief enemies.

Plague A devastating and deadly disease that moves swiftly through a large group.

Prophets Special people chosen by the Mighty One to speak His Words to His people.

Sacrifice Something of great value that is offered up to the Mighty One, usually as part of a ritual of repentance or thanksgiving. Ancient pagans also made sacrifices to their nature gods, to try to please them.

Sarah Wife of Abraham, and mother of Isaac.

Sin (see *iniquities*)

Sir Wyvern Pugilist Author and Dragon Slayer Extraordinaire (often attacked by Braggen).

Tabernacle Another word for "tent," it is the name of the Mighty One's own tent that stood at the center of the Israelites' camp in the desert. It served as the Mighty One's portable temple, in which His presence remained with the people.

Trinity, the (see *Mysterious Three*)

Twelve Tribes of Israel The descendants of the twelve sons of Jacob/Israel. Their offspring were so many, they became twelve great tribes.

Un-Parallelus Without equal (from Latin).

Ur, City of Abraham and Sarah's hometown, on the River Euphrates.

Worship To bow in adoration before the Mighty One, acknowledging that He is Lord of All.

Zechariah One of the prophets in Epeisódion I, he spoke many words from the Mighty One. Also the name of John the Baptist's father (Epeisódion II).

A LIST OF COMMON AND NOTORIOUS DRAGON SPECIES

Avarus	Cringe Liver	Rendagon
Bilgewater	Frantix	Slackbottom
Bogs	Golgoth	Snuffwick
Braggen	Malefactor	Stinkmouth
Breathbane	Morhgall	Youserpin
Bucephalus	Nemecyst	

To learn more about these malicious monsters and how to thwart their vicious attacks (plus neutralize their absolutely putrid, exceedingly loathsome and revolting breath), read my most excellent book *Dragon Slayers: The Essential Training Guide for Young Dragon Fighters, Based Wholly on the Practices of the Great Dragon Slayers of Old and the Wisdom of Their* Ancient Manual.

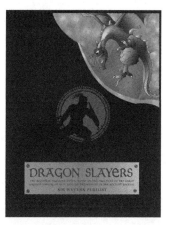

SIR WYVERN PUGILIST
ISBN: 978-1-55725-684-3 • $23.99, Leather look

GALILEE

*Sea of
Galilee*

NAZARETH

*The Great Sea
(Mediterranean)*

SAMARIA

River Jordan

JERUSALEM

BETHLEHEM

*Dead
Sea*

JUDEAN WILDERNESS

JUDAH
(JUDEA)

EGYPT

THE LAND OF
PROMISE IN THE
TIME OF JESUS